CW00819678

First published in Grea
by The Simple

Authors: Asim Khan & Toyris Miah
Cover design & illustrations by: Anisa Mohammed
Editing by: Malika Kahn

Book design by The Simple Seerah Ltd.

Published by The Simple Seerah Ltd.

Printed by Bartham Press
www.barthampress.com

Printed in Great Britain

ISBN 978-1-7399095-0-5

www.simpleseerah.com | info@simpleseerah.com

The Simple Seerah Ltd. Kemp House,
152-160 City Road, London, EC1V 2NX

Stealing Is Forbidden

In Islam, stealing is considered to be a terrible crime and there are clear commandments which tell us not to do so. It is even considered a sin to buy products if you know they are stolen. With this in mind, we kindly ask you to ensure that you do not copy, scan, photograph or record the contents of this book in any shape or form and then share it with others.

If you receive a PDF of this book, please do not share it with others, as the PDF is stolen property.

You are more than welcome to lend or gift your own physical copy of this book to anyone of your choosing.

To purchase a genuine copy of this book please visit www.simpleseerah.com

If you are unable to purchase your own copy, please contact us via our website and we will send you a copy (terms and conditions apply). Please see our website for further details.

Acknowledgements

The Prophet ﷺ said:
"The best of charity is when a Muslim gains knowledge,
then teaches it to a fellow Muslim."
Sunan Ibn Majah, Vol. 1, Book 1, Hadith 243

Alhamdulillah. We thank Allah for allowing us to produce this book and for instilling the idea into our hearts and minds. Any good that is in this book and achieved from this work is solely credited to Allah (swt) as all that is good and pure is from Allah. Any mistakes and errors are from us and we seek forgiveness from Allah and from our brothers and sisters.

Thousands of people contributed to the production of this book and we pray that Allah rewards you all immensely for your support and contributions. We would like to especially thank those who sponsored either half of a chapter or an entire chapter as a form of Sadaqah Jariyah (continuous charity) on behalf of themselves and their loved ones, whose names are printed on the sponsors' mosaic; may it be accepted from you, Ameen!

We would also like to acknowledge the hard work and support from the following individuals and groups:

The East London Mosque & London Muslim Centre, LaunchGood, Pilgrim, IlmFeed and Ilm Tours.

Zain Luqman Miah, Sania Kibria, Syed Hiru Eesa, Abdullah Al-Mubin and Mostaque Koyes.

Contents

Mufti Menk Foreword

All praise is due to Allah Almighty, and may peace and salutations be upon His Final Messenger, Muhammad ﷺ.

Just as important as it is for every Muslim to understand the Qur'an and use it as a compass for their everyday life, it is also important for us to understand the life of the Messenger of Allah, Muhammad ﷺ, through whom Allah sent humanity the Qur'an.

Why did Allah choose the Prophet Muhammad, what was so special about him, and what made him different from the rest of the people of that time and today? All these questions and more are addressed by Ustadh Asim Khan in this much-needed book on the *Seerah*.

Appropriately titled as "The Simple Seerah", one of the main objectives of this book is to make it easy for the young generation of Muslims today to understand and learn from the life of the Prophet ﷺ. The novel-like language and storytelling structure used throughout the book is easy and engaging for most youngsters and even adults. Combined with the brilliant illustrations, you're transported to ancient Makkah to witness the trials and challenges of the early Muslims.

Due to the distractions of today, especially from the entertainment industry, many young Muslims are growing up idolizing fictitious characters or singers who display the most vulgar behaviour. To help tackle this, "The Simple Seerah" focuses on key events and individuals from the early days of Islam to remind Muslims that we have our own real-life heroes!

To ensure that every event mentioned in this book is genuine, Ustadh Asim Khan has only mentioned events about the Prophet that can be backed up from the classical books of *Seerah* like Ibn Ishaq, Ibn Hisham, and Ibn Kathir. This is incredibly reassuring for all of us as it ensures what we are reading is accurate and not fiction.

I ask Allah Almighty to grant the distinguished authors greater acceptance. May He bless their families, students, and friends who supported them throughout the journey of producing "The Simple Seerah".

Mufti Menk

Our Principles

Everyone loves a good story, it's just that we don't call them stories anymore, we call them movies and dramas. In a world of wizards, *Hobbits*, *Jedis* and *Marvel* superheroes, you could easily be led to believe that the best stories are those written (or filmed) in our times, right? But what if I were to tell you that in your hands right now lies the greatest story ever to be told? A story like no other—a story that is an inspiration to all of humanity?

This is a story of how an orphan child who lived in the deserts of Arabia fourteen-hundred years ago became the most powerful and beloved human being to ever walk the face of this earth—a story of a true superhero. This is the story of none other than the Prophet Muhammad ﷺ, which is known as *Seerah* in Arabic.

Although many books have been written about his blessed life, this book is the first of its kind. It lifts the raw narrative as told in classical *Seerah* literature, which spans over a thousand years, and translates it into a flowing, descriptive and enchanting narrative that is engaging for both young and old.

Here are some of the key principles we followed in producing this ground-breaking work:

1. Every quote of the Prophet ﷺ and Companions found in this book is a direct historical narration taken from the classical works of *Seerah*.[1]

2. Readers are strongly encouraged to say *sallallahu alayhi wassalam* (May the peace and blessing of Allah be upon him) wherever they see the Prophet's name mentioned.

3. No event or incident about the Prophet ﷺ falls into the realm of fiction. There are, however, added details that are extrapolations based on the raw *Seerah* narrative, verses from the Qur'an, and other Prophetic narrations (Hadith) as found in the classical sources. These details are there to help transport the reader to the time of the Prophet ﷺ by adding ambience and environment to each scene.

---

[1] See Endnotes for the complete list

4. This book is not meant to be a comprehensive narrative of the *Seerah*. The details we believe are the most inspirational to the younger audience have been given priority due to the nature of this book.

5. This work is based on the most authoritative classical sources in the *Seerah* literature. A full list can be found in the Bibliography and Endnotes.

Lastly, the Prophet ﷺ presented Islam to the people of the time using the language of the time. Here we are trying to relay the message of the *Seerah* to the people of today using the language of today while retaining the everlasting message and values of the beloved of Allah.

May the eternal peace and blessings of Allah be upon him.

Asim Khan
Toyris Miah

THE SIMPLE
SEERAH

Asim Khan & Toyris Miah

Illustrated By: Anisa Mohammed

Edited By: Malika Kahn

Chapter 1
Dawn of A Legacy

Hushed murmurs filled the air. The tension in the room grew in intensity. His presence, even in a state of sickness, warmed the room. His wives hovered close by, ever vigilant and ready to tend to the one they held dear. They noticed that he kept asking: "Where shall I be tomorrow? Where shall I be tomorrow?"

Realizing that he wanted to know when he could be with his wife Aisha, they all agreed that he should be moved to her house to be nursed back to health. They arranged for it without delay. Before long, the Prophet lay there quietly with his head resting on Aisha's chest, his forehead wrapped tightly with a cloth to help calm the pain. The fever was so severe that she could feel the heat radiating through his blessed clothes. He was now too weak to lead the prayers, but the people of Madinah seemed to have considered his sickness as just a passing inconvenience. Something minor that he would recover from in due time. And so, whenever the time for prayer arrived, they would patiently wait for him in the mosque, hoping for a glimpse of the man they all loved.

The Prophet's Companions clutched at any straw of hope, interpreting every small action as a positive sign of recovery, like when the Prophet staggered over to the inside window of his home to peer into the mosque. As he stood there gazing in, the Companions all felt his presence, and their attention began wavering even though they were standing in prayer. The Prophet felt deeply saddened by the inability to go sit with his Companions and longed to lead them in prayer. At the same time, he was grateful beyond measure, particularly conscious of the favours that Allah had bestowed upon him.

Although his life may well have been coming to an end, he felt a profound sense of appreciation for being granted the opportunity to do so much good in his lifetime, more than he could have imagined—more than any other prophet before him. However, the Muslim community appeared to have found the idea of his death so unbearable and frightening that they failed to read the signs correctly—everyone except Abu Bakr, that is.

8 June 632

Aisha felt that there was something different about the Prophet. He was lying more heavily in her lap. She could tell by the gentle flickering of his eyelids that he seemed to be pulled in and out of consciousness. Still, she did not quite realize what was happening. Aisha wrung out a strip of wet cloth, the droplets gently resounding as they hit the remaining water in the container. She leaned over the Prophet, close enough to feel the warmth of his breath on her cheek, only to hear him repeatedly murmur, "Truly, I desire the most Elevated Companion in Paradise."

The Prophet's breathing slowed with every breath he struggled to take. Still Aisha held him tightly, praying he could hold on, but soon a stillness overtook him, and he lay heavy in her arms.

Like an arrow piercing through the air, the news travelled quickly through the oasis of Madinah. When it reached Abu Bakr, he hurried back from one of his homes outside the city, heading straight to his daughter. Raising the curtain with one arm, he stepped into the small room, making his presence known with a soft greeting to Aisha. Her response was barely audible. A moment of understanding passed between the two. Abu Bakr took one look at the Prophet—his best friend since the age of fifteen—leaned over, and while holding back the tears, kissed his face to bid him farewell.

"You smell as fragrant right now as you did while alive," he uttered, managing a thin, quivering smile as he gazed upon his dearest friend. His heart ached, and he could only imagine the pain felt by his daughter, whose cheeks were stained with silent tears.

Abu Bakr breathed in, closed his eyes, and then with a sense of resolve, he straightened his turban. As he stood at the doorway into the mosque, he pushed back an avalanche of emotions and began the process of accepting the decree of Allah. Death was a fact of life, its time appointed for all creation, even the very best of them. With a sense of purpose fuelling his steps, Abu Bakr walked into the mosque where he found the Companion Umar addressing the gathering crowds. Umar absolutely refused to believe that the Prophet had passed away.

"I swear by God the Messenger is not dead!" he passionately argued, long arms thrashing the air animatedly. "He will certainly return to us just like Moses came back to his people after forty nights."

Abu Bakr, realizing how extremely delicate the situation was, knew that he would have to be gentle but firm with the people, starting with Umar. He walked over to this towering personality, and, reaching out to hold his arm, he said, "Gently, O Umar."

Yet Umar would not and could not stop talking. All that Abu Bakr could do was step forward quietly, the solemn expression on his face and composure of his body indicating that he was about to make an important announcement. The crowd fell silent, recognizing that the man who was closest to the Prophet was about to speak. What followed was news that drowned out the noise of anything else; every sound and every thought froze in that moment. By the time Abu Bakr had finished his speech, Umar had fallen to the ground, his legs unable to support not just his towering body but the heaviness of the truth.

The news of the Prophet's passing rocked the city of Madinah. It was the single biggest crisis that they had ever faced—and they had seen many in their time. Until this moment, Prophet Muhammad had guided their every step. He had shown them a vision of hope through a faith they could never have imagined. To the Muslims, he was as much of a strong leader as he was a caring advisor and a noble teacher. He was their direct connection to Divine Revelation, to Allah. How then were they supposed to continue without him?

With the wound of grief still fresh, a feeling of numbness and hopelessness fell over the Muslims as they struggled for a sense of direction. Deep down, the Companions feared this marked the end of an era. However, Allah had not willed for this to be the end, rather, it was only the beginning of the legacy that the Prophet left behind for the Muslims then, the Muslims of today, and the Muslims of the future.

The Companions had each gravitated towards the Prophet. Even though some had, at first, wilfully denied him or were amongst his fiercest opponents, they found themselves drawn to his message. And even before his prophethood, he had won the loyalty of hearts by simply being himself: sincere and kind. What made Muhammad so highly regarded, so deeply loved? The Companion, Zayd, was faced with this question when he was still a young boy.

Kidnapped from his family when he was just a child, Zayd was sold into slavery and brought to Makkah. At ten years old, he found himself in the care of Muhammad's family. What he expected would be a time of great trauma ended up being the opposite. This household was *different*. He realized this each time he went to the market where he crossed paths with other slaves whose masters were the cause of their miserable faces or throbbing scars. Young Zayd would often return from errands saddened by what he saw, but when greeted by the smiling face of Muhammad, his heart swelled with gratefulness. Although he missed his family, the pain was soothed by the warm meals and smiles he received in what he came to regard as his new home.

Unbeknownst to Zayd, his father, Haritha, had never given up looking for him. Haritha made it his mission to find his missing child, and after many years, discovered that Zayd was still alive, living in Makkah. He journeyed across the desert to rescue his son, but his reunion was met with an unexpected response: Zayd refused to leave.

"Why do you wish to stay with this man instead of me, your real father!?" he asked, stunned at his son's behaviour. He scrutinized young Zayd, who appeared at ease and well cared for despite being a slave, his brown skin shining with a healthy glow.

The young boy looked over to Muhammad for instruction, but he merely signalled to Zayd that he was free to choose his own path. Undisguised admiration filled the boy's eyes. Zayd turned to his father, responding that he had a special feeling about this man. With conviction, he said, "I would not leave Muhammad's side for anything the world has to offer."[1]

Little did Zayd know that many years later, Muhammad would become a Prophet and would not only entrust him to command the entire Muslim army but also teach him how to raise an outstanding son, Usamah, who would go on to reach a position of greatness beyond even his father. Young Zayd's enduring love and loyalty were shared by all the Prophet's Companions, male and female. To this day, the legacy of Prophet Muhammad continues to be a source of deep admiration, unwavering respect, and surprise.

When the setting sun concluded the heavy day of heartbreak, the sky held onto some of the glow until the call to prayer greeted the people of Madinah at dawn. They knew then that even though Muhammad was no longer with them, the Lord of Muhammad never dies. The message would live on.

To this day, Islam continues to be the fastest-growing religion in the world. No other individual in history can claim the same level of success of their mission. How did an orphan boy who had never learned to read or write not only challenge a culture, but replace it with a whole new way of life that brought peace and unity to an otherwise violent environment? What was it about his character that earned the respect and allegiance of people from various walks of life long before his prophethood? To understand how an orphan from the deserts of Arabia became the most powerful and loved man in the world, his influence traversing the passage of time, it is only right that we get to know Muhammad and his life in the intimate detail presented in this book.

Chapter 2
A Rocky Start

In the year 570 CE, more than a thousand years ago, something happened that changed the world. History is like a string of endless beads, and nestled in between is one shimmering pearl clearly distinguishable from all others; that is the day Muhammad was born to Amina in the arid desert of Makkah. Even the year itself was distinct, for Allah sent the people of Makkah a miracle that set it apart from all others.

The Quraysh—the people who lived in Makkah—referred to this time as the Year of the Elephant because of the large Abyssinian army that came to attack the city. The army was led by an ambitious general named Abraha, who wanted revenge because an Arab from Makkah had defiled his grand cathedral in Yemen. Abraha brought with him a number of magnificent and imposing African elephants. These elephants, trained to smash through any object in their path, were towering, heavy-footed creatures that made the ground quiver and quake as they marched towards the city. The sweltering heat and dry air did nothing to deter their path. The goal was to destroy the Ka'bah, and the Abyssinian army was determined to succeed. In fact, because of the formidable creatures at the forefront of their ranks, they felt that victory was guaranteed; the Quraysh wouldn't stand a chance.

When the Quraysh spotted the army in the distance, they felt helpless. They decided then and there to abandon any ideas of putting up a fight, having neither the weapons nor the strength to defeat this ferocious army. The situation looked hopeless as the enemy reached the city's outskirts until suddenly, the advancing elephants came to a mysterious standstill – a total halt. The General yelled out instructions all the way from his carriage mounted on top of the lead elephant. Bewildered, the troops dashed around as they tried to figure out what was going on.

The elephants refused to take a single step further. The warriors knew that these great beasts were strong; they could go on for days without water, for miles without resting. There was absolutely no logical reason for them to have stopped. Yet, no matter how much the warriors pushed or pulled or thrashed them, the elephants wouldn't budge. Desperate whips cracked and ropes snapped. The sound of the elephants trumpeting in protest echoed throughout the streets of Makkah. Increasingly frustrated, the General ordered the army to continue ahead. Then, a miracle unfolded, something the Quraysh had never seen before, not even in their wildest imagination.

To protect the Ka'bah, Allah unleashed a flock of birds so vast that they overshadowed the skies. The small birds circled in the air before swooping down upon Abraha's army, pelting them with a shower of stones raining from their claws and beaks. Even though each stone was as small as a chickpea, it was enough to terrify the army. The pebbles were launched with such velocity that they pierced through coats of armour. Each stone found its mark, and as soon as the warriors were struck, their flesh began to rot, either frighteningly fast or sickeningly slow.[2] Frantic and afraid, the entire army fled in retreat, leaving behind their weapons, war flags, and a story that would be recounted for generations.

This astonishing event was a huge favour from Allah to protect the holy city of Makkah and one of the incredible ways in which He was preparing the world to receive the new Prophet. The Final Prophet. The time had arrived for Muhammad to enter the world.

§

Amina had realized early on that her pregnancy was out of the ordinary—her baby was different. She had many experiences that were not easy to share with others nor something she could simply explain away. One night she heard mysterious voices saying, "You carry in your womb the leader of all people."

Sometimes, it was as if she could see lights shining from her belly like shooting stars that stretched as far as Syria—hundreds of miles away—illuminating its castles.[3] This was a sign from Allah about the great things to come in the life of Muhammad, similar to the dream He inspired Prophet Joseph (Yusuf) to have as a child about the sun, moon, and eleven stars all bowing down to him, symbolizing the path of nobility that lay ahead.

Sadly, while still a baby inside his mother's womb, Muhammad's father Abdullah passed away, making him an orphan child. Muhammad never had the opportunity to see his father beyond piecing together an image in his mind based on stories he would hear when he was a little older. Being fatherless was seen as a great shame amongst the Arabs. Thankfully, his mother took great care of him. Amina saw to her infant son with tenderness and love. As her only child, she treasured him and had high hopes for his future.

On the seventh day after Muhammad's birth, his grandfather Abdul Muttalib invited family and friends to celebrate the arrival of his grandson. Abdul Muttalib was the father of Abdullah, whom he had loved very much, so it came as no surprise that the offspring of his late son would hold a special place in his heart. Abdul Muttalib made sure that the very best sheep were slaughtered in preparation for the grand feast to honour and officially welcome his beloved grandson into the tribe. The heat of midday found guests socializing beneath the welcoming shade of a wide communal tent. Some people stood, showing off their best robes, while others reclined against the plump cushions scattered on top of the deep red and olive-green carpets spread on the ground. Platters of fresh fruit were served, and traditional tea was poured. Everyone was having such fun, attracting the attention of passers-by who proceeded to join in as well. Suddenly, Abdul Muttalib said something that caught the gathering by surprise.

With a great big smile on his face, he commanded the attention of his guests and proudly announced, "I have decided to name this child ... Muhammad!"

The Praised One...? The people were startled by his choice.

His enthusiastic announcement was met with an awkward silence which was quickly broken by someone who shouted out: "Why have you chosen such an unusual name for this child?"

Some of the attendees directed annoyed looks at the boldness of this man, hoping his audacity had not offended their esteemed host. Abdul Muttalib merely smiled, pleased with this question, for whether or not someone had asked, he was full well intending to shed light on his reason for selecting a name not commonly known to his people.

"I have hope that he will be praised by God in the Heavens and by His creation on the Earth," he replied with great confidence, holding up the baby and then hugging him closely.

Abdul Muttalib was a powerful man, being the leader of a great tribe, and so the people, not wanting to upset him, simply smiled politely and continued to enjoy the feast. The crowd's lack of enthusiasm did nothing to dim his own. The proud grandfather looked down affectionately at the baby cradled in his arms. Abdul Muttalib's sentiments and wishes for his grandson were incredibly fitting in the grand scheme of things, but not even he could have guessed just how loved and praised this child would eventually become to the world.

In the months that followed, Amina lovingly cared for her infant son until it was time for him to leave Makkah. It was the tradition of the people of Makkah to give their young children to milk-mothers who lived in the deserts away from the noisy city. These women would nurse and raise the babies until they were healthy and fit to return home. Unlike in the city of Makkah, life was a lot simpler in the open desert, despite the harsher climate. The landscape was dry and merciless, the hot sun beating down on the sand, which stretched for miles on end. So why then would anyone send their young child to live in the desert? As strange as it may sound, the practice had its benefits: the children would spend the first few years of their lives soaking in the clean desert air, being close to nature, and hearing the purest version of the Arabic language spoken around them. Honour, pride, loyalty, independence, defiance of hardship—these were the core values of Bedouin culture that the Quraysh hoped would rub off on their young.

A woman named Halima agreed to take Muhammad and look after him. She would send him back to Makkah occasionally to visit his mother. In those years spent raising him, Halima and her family noticed that many blessings had entered their lives the moment Muhammad joined their household. Their camels and sheep provided more milk than ever before, and despite experiencing a drought, they were never short of food.

One day, when Muhammad was around four years old, he went to play in the desert with two other boys. They raced beyond the pair of date palms decorating the edge of the oasis. As they were playing, something strange and incredible happened. Out of nowhere, two tall figures dressed from head to toe in brilliant white robes approached the boys. They appeared to be almost gliding. Suddenly and without warning, they grabbed Muhammad. He yelled, not knowing who they were. Terrified, the two boys turned on their heels, kicking up clouds of sand as they raced to Halima's tent.

Muhammad tried to break free but to no avail. Within a few seconds, the mysterious figures did something to make him fall into a deep sleep. While Muhammad was unconscious, his eyes fully closed, the tall figures, who were in fact angels, quickly cut open the young boy's chest. They took out his heart and carefully placed it in a golden bowl where they washed it with special water from a well called Zam Zam. Then, they removed a little black piece attached to his heart. As they threw it away, explaining, "This was the piece of your heart that Satan, the devil, wanted for himself."

During this whole procedure, Muhammad did not feel a thing; it was completely painless. After removing the black speck, the angels carefully placed his heart back inside his chest. By some miracle, his chest closed up, leaving behind only a faint line that looked like an old scar.[4] The mark was similar to someone who had stitches after hurting themselves, a tell-tale sign of the incident. The real miracle, however, was the long-lasting effect this procedure would have on Muhammad. It would strengthen his heart to bear the weight of God's Revelation, protect him from the evil whispers of the devil, and enable him to travel through the Heavens and beyond with an angel by his side.

Meanwhile, back at Halima's home, the goats bleated in agitation, startled by all the commotion. Their ears twitched as they heard Halima urging the boys to speak. "What is the matter?" she asked once again.

The two boys were almost tripping over their words out of fear as they tried to explain what happened. The older one cleared his throat nervously before spluttering out, "It's Muhammad. He's been t-t-taken away!"

Without a moment to waste, Halima and the family all ran out to try and find Muhammad. When they reached him, they found him alone with no one else in sight. He was awake but was not screaming or crying as Halima had expected. Instead, he sat silently, his usually vibrant face pale as if drained of all its colour. Halima rushed to pull him into a hug, resting her chin on his head. She stroked his forehead, which was cold and clammy to the touch. Then she pulled back, holding his shoulders as she took a good look at the visibly shaken boy. Sensing that something strange had indeed taken place, she felt her fears rise.

What would Amina say if something terrible had happened to her son while I was supposed to be looking after him? She worried.

Halima wanted to return him safely, feeling that being with his family might be what was best for him. Immediately, she prepared to take Muhammad back to his mother. After many hours of travel, they arrived in Makkah. When she reached the home of Amina, she told the startled mother that she could no longer take care of Muhammad. Amina was taken aback by the sudden, unexpected return of her child and wanted to know why.

When Halima told Amina the truth about what happened back in the desert, she was amazed to find that Amina was not frightened nor angry. Instead, Muhammad's mother was calm and unflustered by this astonishing news. With a cool gaze, Amina reassured her.

"Don't worry, don't be afraid. My son is protected by Allah." She placed her hand on her tummy. "When he was born, there was a light shining from here that reached all the way to Syria."

Halima found that she could believe this story, knowing all too well that extraordinary, unexplainable happenings and Muhammad's presence seemed to go hand in hand. She looked at the young boy who had been patiently waiting, gently holding onto his mother's cloak while the women conversed. Halima smiled faintly. She and her family would miss him. She was certain that even the animals that he played with in the village and its surroundings would miss him too. With a heartfelt goodbye, they parted ways, and Muhammad was back in the care of his mother. At least, for a little while.

The path to greatness and success may have a rocky start. The Prophet Muhammad had to grow up without a father as an orphan child. However, this helped him become strong and resilient—qualities that we all need to achieve great things in life. Moreover, having to grow up as an orphan gave him the ability to empathize with the weaker and less privileged in society. This made him more sensitive to the feelings of others, more compassionate, and all the more willing to help those in need.

Chapter 3
Learning The Ropes

Now back in Makkah, young Muhammad stayed with his mother for two years. When he was six, Amina decided to take her son on a trip to meet the members of her family who lived in the city called Yathrib. It was arranged that they would tag along with a trade caravan heading in that direction. Amina and Muhammad set out on the journey with the devoted assistance of an older female servant. The caravan, mostly consisting of hearty merchants and proud camels, crossed the deserts of Arabia in a long, narrow formation. In the evenings, the camp would sit cross-legged around fires that flickered with warmth and light. The merchants enjoyed having a young one amongst them and would often rope Muhammad in to doing little tasks, which he all too gladly assisted with. On a few occasions, Amina heard remarks about her son's graceful manners, to which she smiled privately to herself, watching as he darted across the camp to help dish out bread.

The generous amongst the travellers would divide their food and share blankets to shield others from the cold bite of the night. In this way, the travellers depended on each other to make the journey through the rocky mountain paths and shifting dunes a little bit easier. It took more than a week until they reached their destination safely. On that evening, young Muhammad first set his eyes upon the city of Yathrib, unaware that it would one day become known as *Madinatu Nabi*, The City of the Prophet. *His* city. Amongst the Jewish Tribes that lived there, some awaited the arrival of a new prophet, not knowing that he had already crossed paths with them as a little boy with his arms around his mother, resting his chin on her shoulder as he gazed with fascination at the stars speckling the vast night sky.

Amina received a warm welcome, and finally, Muhammad got to meet his aunts and uncles. The climate in Yathrib was cooler than in Makkah, a few degrees more pleasant, and so most days were spent outdoors during this season. Resting beneath sturdy date palms, exploring the rows of trees in the farmers' groves, and tagging along to the bustling marketplace,

Muhammad would have remembered these days in Yathrib as joyous had things not taken a tragic turn. On their way back home, Amina fell ill. She didn't have the energy to travel on. They soon neared a place called Abwa, a distance outside the city of Yathrib. Amina leaned onto her servant for support, her condition having worsened as she exerted herself to carry on. In this little village, Amina drew her last breath after a final, feverish gaze at her precious child.[5] At the tender age of six, Muhammad had now lost both his mother and father. Little did he know that the city he would grow up associating with pain and loss would one day become a source of hope and glory. Nonetheless, the pain of having to bury his mother sat deep within him for the rest of his life.

When older, the Prophet would make a point of stopping at Abwa to stand beside the grave of his mother out of love and longing. Sometimes his visits were accompanied by his Companions. On one particular occasion, he stopped at Abwa, followed by a group of around a thousand Companions. The mood fell sombre as they realized that this was the burial place of the Prophet's mother. Muhammad offered two units of prayer (*salah*) and then stood to address the crowd who sat motionlessly, attention fixated on the face of their Prophet. Tears streamed down his blessed cheeks as he tried to speak through the painful memories of losing his mother.

The Companion by the name of Umar sensed the difficulty the Prophet was experiencing. He stood up to support him. "O Messenger of Allah, what is the matter?" he asked with concern, his usually earnest tone of voice softened with gentleness.

The Prophet's eyes shone with emotion as he spoke. "Just now, I begged Allah to allow me to seek forgiveness for my mother, but He did not permit me..." he revealed, his words heavy, as his mother had not been a Muslim when she died. "But then I sought permission to continue visiting her grave, and He has allowed me that," he continued. "And so I cry these tears in the hope that they will become a source of mercy for her in the Afterlife."[6]

This was something that saddened the Prophet, and since many of the Companions could relate, the sincerity of his emotions touched their hearts.

As a parentless young boy, Muhammad had returned home from Yathrib to the comforting embrace of his grandfather, the wise Abdul Muttalib, who took him under his care. For two years, Muhammad would sit next to his grandfather, chief of the Hashim Tribe, under the shade of the Ka'bah, closely watching how a leader conducted himself and dealt with disputes amongst people. In Makkah, there was no concept of a King's throne, but the Arabs did have a substitute. The tradition was that a special rug, ornate with hues of orange and red, was laid out every day on a slightly raised platform next to the Ka'bah. Only the chief of Quraysh was allowed to sit on it—not even his own sons were afforded that privilege. This was a long-standing tradition until one day, Abdul Muttalib decided to break it.

One afternoon, as the heat began to let up, the locals gathered to rest in the shade of the Ka'bah. They watched the merchants go about their day and, occasionally, smiled pompously at the few pilgrims who stopped to admire the glorious sacred building draped in strips of the finest, colourful fabric sourced from afar. Young Muhammad walked by, noticing his grandfather sitting in his special spot, surrounded by a small group of people. With an innocent smile, he came running, jumping playfully through the crowd before hopping onto the platform to embrace his grandfather. The people gasped. A few hands reached out to pull him down, but Abdul Muttalib signalled to leave the boy alone.

"No one except my grandson Muhammad may sit in this spot," he informed the public. "This boy," he said proudly, holding up the child's hand, "will be very important one day."

It was in this spot that Muhammad observed the wisdom of his grandfather and learned how to lead and engage in diplomacy. Through these interactions, he gained insight into the lives of the rich and the struggles of the poor. In Makkah, tribal feuds and even wars were the rule, not the exception. The young boy would witness many quarrels break out. His grandfather would try to act as judge and jury, but oftentimes things would quickly escalate. Even the simplest of disputes could easily become violent. On one such occasion, Muhammad watched as Abdul Muttalib assumed the role of mediator between two men who had hurriedly arrived, almost elbowing each other as they came to stand before him. The atmosphere was rife with tension as the men exchanged glares.

"Qusay has done it again!" the shortest one proclaimed, thrusting an accusing, skinny finger at the other. "Whenever I take my flock out to graze, he brings his lot to the same areas that I frequent. Each time, I return home to find one or two of my sheep missing. My best ones. It happens too often to be a coincidence, yet he keeps denying it!"

Abdul Muttalib said nothing and waited patiently for the accused to defend himself.

With a dismissive sneer, the man crossed his arms, turning his head skyward. "Please do not flatter yourself, Hathem. Who would go out of their way to take *your* animals?" he scoffed. "The poor creatures are skin and bone, barely any substance."

An offended Hathem clenched his fists. "Then explain to Abdul Muttalib why I recognize some of my own amongst your flock."

"Desperation," was the simple reply. Arrogance rolled off Qusay's tongue as he raised his bushy eyebrows. "Your negligence is no problem of mine, yet you insist on being paid for your so-called losses."

Hathem gasped. Accusations were thrown about, each swearing by this god and that god from amongst the legions of idols that they worshipped, and had Abdul Muttalib not interrupted, fists were about to be thrown as well. It was decided that they would draw lots to settle whether one man was indeed indebted to the other. The men marked a handful of thin twigs, amongst which one represented Qusay, and another represented Hathem. The sticks would be shuffled, and the one Abdul Muttalib selected would resolve their dispute. This was the best option he could suggest, knowing that fate was the only thing that could put this topic to rest. The sticks dictated that Hathem did not have to pay Qusay and the men were advised to graze their flocks separately. Despite all this, the issue was not entirely resolved, as young Muhammad would come to know. Time would find Hathem's flock shrinking in size while Qusay's would only grow in number, skinny sheep trotting amongst the plumper ones. Hathem would eventually give up, thinking to himself that there was only so many times he could muster up the energy to bother Abdul Muttalib with the same old grievances.

There was no true sense of justice, Muhammad began to see. The young boy came to understand that it was really the law of the jungle that governed the land, and those from the most powerful tribe would call the shots. As for the poor and weak, life was brutal to say the least. Thoughts of this nature passed through his innocent mind as he witnessed the daily dilemmas, but he kept them to himself, at least for the time being.

The days of tagging along, listening and learning, only lasted two short years. When he was eight years old, Muhammad lost his esteemed grandfather, bringing their remarkable relationship to a shattering end. He wept many tears for his grandfather but was comforted by the countless vivid, fond memories of the legend that was Abdul Muttalib which he could cling onto for many years to come. All these losses shaped Muhammad's outlook on life from an early age, teaching him that there were no guarantees in this temporary world and that only God was in control of life and death.

On his deathbed, Abdul Muttalib had entrusted Muhammad into the care of his son, Abu Talib. Abu Talib and his wife Fatimah loved their nephew dearly, leaving little doubt in the boy's mind that they would sacrifice for him as much as, if not more than they would for their own children. Though his uncle would take great care of him, becoming his fiercest supporter when he would one day become a Prophet, during this particular time, Abu Talib was struggling financially. As soon as he was able to, Muhammad took it upon himself to search for a job so that he could help support his dear uncle's family.

The deserts of Arabia were no playground. The landscape was harsh, the ground scorched by sunlight, and every so often, a violent sandstorm would unleash itself upon anyone who dared to wander the open spaces. The heavy silence was deafening, occasionally broken by the screeching of eagles or the howling of wild dogs. It was in this environment where Muhammad found a job as a shepherd, tasked with the responsibility of tending to the sheep of farmers for a small wage. He would wake up early, just as dawn broke, before heading out to the old farmers who would hand over their sheep for him to take along the desert hills surrounding Makkah. Muhammad would then have to lead the flock deep into the valleys for grazing and then bring them back before sunset, every one of them safe and sound, their bellies full.

Being a shepherd was no simple task. Many dangers prowled the deserts beyond the city. Horrible wild dogs and sneaky hyenas were always looking for an easy meal. Their sharp, iron-grip fangs could devour a wandering sheep quicker than it could bleat for help. Then there was the hard work involved in searching the valleys and hills for bushes and grass for the sheep to eat while making sure that none got lost or dehydrated in the process. All this effort carried with it a variety of useful skills and experience that would, later on, shine through Muhammad's character.

Tending to the sheep fostered within him a sense of responsibility. In this manner, Muhammad, as a youth working as a humble shepherd, acquired an array of leadership skills in the unlikeliest of environments. Carefully herding a flock of fifty lively sheep from place to place nurtured within him the patience of a saint. Protecting them from the dangers of the desert sharpened his wit and intelligence. Spending time alone, watching the sheep graze peacefully, gave him moments to reflect over the signs of Allah rarely noticed in the hustle and bustle of a city. He watched as the sun-seared desert rock released the heat of the day into the cooled evening air. The way the shrubs tilted as if following the movement of the sun as the hours drifted by. The finer details of life became apparent, fuelling his appreciation. He would later come to rely on the qualities these experiences instilled in him as a Prophet of God and a leader of people. Indeed, when he eventually became one, he would tell his followers: "Every one of you is a shepherd!" Everyone was a leader in one way or another.

When he became a teenager, another form of training presented itself. Something far more dangerous and difficult than working as a shepherd.

Muhammad would often spend time with his uncles, Hamza and Abbas. Hamza trained him how to use the weapons of war. As a man of great stature and strength, Hamza was known for being an exceptionally skilled swordsman and wrestler. However, it was archery that his nephew came to excel in. The young boy gave every promise of becoming an excellent bowman, something his late father would have loved to see. In these years of Muhammad's youth, the Quraysh was not involved in any serious war except for one occasional and intermittent conflict. A man from the Kinanah Tribe had treacherously murdered a man from the Amir Tribe and had taken refuge in an impregnable fortress in the city of Khaybar. What happened next followed the typical senseless pattern of violence the deserts of Arabia were known for: honour demanded revenge, which led to counter revenge, and down the spiral of pointless killing they all plunged.

The tribe of the murdered man attacked Kinanah—the tribe of the murderer—which caused the Quraysh to become involved, being allies of Kinanah. The conflict dragged on for three years in which there were only five days of actual fighting. Grudges between the tribes ran deeper than the well of Zam Zam. One day, some men from the Kinanah Tribe were chased down by men from the Amir Tribe. Under the blazing heat of midday, they wrestled and howled and cursed in a brutal display beneath the bright, blue sky that stretched out above them. After some fierce fighting, the tribe of Kinanah retreated into the sanctuary of Makkah, a place recognized by all Arabs as so holy that no fighting on its land was allowed.

The next day, Amir tribesmen violated this sacred law. They carried with them daggers concealed in their waist-cloths, and when passing by their sworn enemies, they drew blood. Fighting erupted within the city. Those who did not have weapons grabbed the poles that secured tents and sprung into the fray. Injustices on both sides increased with each casualty, and in that moment, the sacred law was long forgotten. For this reason, the conflict was dubbed "The Unholy War".

At the time, the head of the Hashim Tribe was Zubayr. Like Abu Talib, he was the full brother of Muhammad's father. Zubayr and Abu Talib took their nephew with them to one of the first battles. Muhammad, only fifteen years old, found himself dressed in armour as he entered the battlefield with his uncles. Although he was too young to fight, he was allowed to help in other ways. For the most part, he was kept protected at the rear of the army, though each time he spotted an opportunity, he broke away.

Moving skilfully out of the safety net of formation, young Muhammad shielded himself from the incoming volley of arrows descending upon them from the enemies' side. Quickly, he tracked down these arrows that missed their mark, handing them over to his uncles to shoot back at the opponents.[7] At the end of the day, his leather armour boasted scratches and dents much like those who were on the frontlines.

During one of the subsequent battles, Quraysh and their allies were suffering a heavy loss, and Muhammad was allowed to participate fully. In this battle, he showed his skill as a bowman. In the thick of the fighting, amidst all the clamouring, Muhammad remained composed as he drew his first arrow back and then sent it accelerating ahead with remarkable precision—after all, he was trained by the best warrior in Makkah. The battle reached its climax, the fighters on both sides drenched in sweat and grime. Nearing exhaustion, they pushed hard to end things. With his supply of arrows at the ready, Muhammad would reach behind him to draw, release, and repeat. One arrow quickly after the other, he kept the momentum going even when he was forced to change his position. His quick thinking and bravery earned the praise of his comrades, some of whom were seasoned archers impressed at this young man's abilities.

It was through these events that Muhammad not only developed the skillset of a warrior but also became aware of the total lack of a system of law by which a victim of crime—like the man from the Amir Tribe who was wrongly killed three years ago—might obtain justice. These incidents troubled his mind and got him thinking of ways to prevent the same thing from happening again. It seemed as though tribal solidarity encouraged bravery and selflessness, but much like a gang mentality, it operated only within the context of one's own tribe, with no concern for outsiders. More and more questions about his people and their ways began to surface in his mind, for which he had no real answers. For now, though, his reputation as an ambitious, brave, and honest young man of Makkah was beginning to take shape. The future was looking bright.

When Allah wants goodness to enter the world, He creates the means that lead to it. Oftentimes those Allah chooses to be the means of change do not realize it as Allah's plan is subtle and delicate. We see how as a boy Muhammad was strengthened by having to overcome the loss of both parents and then his beloved grandfather. His time working as a shepherd taught him patience, leadership, and watchfulness. Even before he entered this world, the Almighty had chosen to destroy the army from Abyssinia who came to demolish the city he would be born in. Slowly but surely, Allah was creating the means through which humanity would receive their Prophet bearing the gift of Revelation.

Chapter 4
Soul Searching

The purity of Muhammad's character grew strikingly apparent as he reached adulthood. By his twenties, he was well-known and respected by the Quraysh. Even the elders would refer to him as *al-Amin*, the

Trustworthy. Before departing on long journeys, merchants would visit him to leave their money and personal valuables in his care while they were away. His courtesy and sincerity took root in the minds of those who crossed paths with him, forming a lasting impression such that when his name arose in conversation, it was guaranteed that something praiseworthy would be said about the fair young man from the Hashim Tribe. Trusted and admired by his people, Muhammad fulfilled the roles required of him with diligence and care, being very much involved in society. Yet, anyone who cared to look closely would notice a reservation about him that distinguished him from his peers and his people. For despite being of service to the Quraysh, Muhammad was quietly distant from their practices.

The jewel in the centre of Makkah was the Ka'bah, the single holiest place on earth. The Quraysh, well aware of its origins, cherished being the custodians of the honourable Ka'bah that was built by Prophet Abraham along with his son Ishmael almost two thousand years before. For many generations, the cube-shaped structure stood tall as an icon symbolizing pure and direct worship to the Maker and Creator of all: Allah. That was until the people of Arabia lost their way and turned, instead, to worshipping idols along with many superstitious beliefs. By the time Muhammad was born, they had transformed the majestic Ka'bah into an eerie temple housing 360 idols. The idols that were not kept inside were dotted around the outside walls, propped up on ornately carved podiums of stone. Where once upon a time Prophet Abraham and his family, dressed in plain white sheets, would walk around this sacred building out of devotion to Allah—a practice continued by millions of believers thereafter—now, inappropriately dressed people danced around it, chanting, clapping, and whistling to their popular idols named Laat, Uzza, and Manaat. Their most revered god of all, Hubal, was etched into heavy stone that was placed higher than any other idol, soullessly overlooking the open-air space of worship. The reeking smell of blood from sheep and camels sacrificed to the idols would often hang in the air amidst the crowds of worshippers as poets would put on performances, and paid entertainers would sing and beat their drums.

Spectacles such as this disturbed Muhammad. His soul simply could not accept that Allah the Almighty would have partners sharing in His kingdom or that such gods, carved by human hands, had the power to answer prayers. He would never bow down to these idols or join in the pagan festivals, even though most of his family would participate. When festivities erupted, the likelihood of running into Muhammad on the streets was very low. Although they noticed this, they chose to overlook it on account of all his other great qualities. Muhammad did, however, join the growing number of businessmen in Makkah by becoming a trader and soon began leading caravans with goods to sell to Syria and Mesopotamia.

Among the Quraysh was a respected and wealthy woman named Khadijah, a distant relative of Muhammad belonging to the powerful tribe of Asad. She was a successful businesswoman also involved in trade, and upon hearing about Muhammad's reputation, sent him a job offer to take a large caravan of goods to Syria. Honoured, Muhammad accepted the offer and set off on the trip accompanied by her trusted servant, Maysara. The extent of Khadijah's fortune soon became apparent to him as he left Makkah at the head of a caravan heavily laden with valuable goods, from rare pottery to ornate carpets. An eye-catching variety of camels trailed out of the city, boasting furs of beige and golden yellow that glimmered in the sunshine. Prized red camels evoked excited murmurs from the swarm of onlookers who came to bid farewell to the men escorting the marvellous caravan on its way to represent the finest of Makkan trade in the competitive environment of Bosra. Muhammad hoped to meet the expectations placed upon the caravan in his charge. He felt confident about the task at hand. Having travelled with his uncle Abu Talib as a child, he was well-accustomed to the route to Bosra, an enchanting Roman city in Syria.

In the weeks of travel that followed, the unrelenting sun seared the sand such that the heat could be felt through the sandals of those walking beside the slow-moving caravan. Even from his horse, Maysara was not spared from the sun's assault, the biting heat causing beads of sweat to trickle down his body. However, whenever his horse steered in the direction of Muhammad's, he would feel a sudden coolness come over him. His mind raced as he looked around in bewilderment for a sign of anything nearby that could be responsible for this relief. Only sand dunes stretched out in all directions as far as his eyes could see. That was until Maysara looked up.

Two enormous clouds hovered over Muhammad, appearing to follow him every time he veered to the right or left.[8] It was happening in such an uncanny way that Maysara thought the heat was making him delirious for thinking that perhaps this strange occurrence had something to do with Muhammad. *But how*...? He wondered, deciding to keep a close eye on this man.

When they arrived at Bosra, they were greeted by the sight of dark buildings made of stone, flanked by pillars that formed elaborate, looming arches. The footfalls of the approaching caravan's camels, horses, and men were drowned out by crowds roaring with cheer as fanfare erupted from the direction of the amphitheatre, the centrepiece of the city, where gladiators fought. The amphitheatre stood tall and bright, an elaborate structure of snow-white alabaster stone that attracted people from far and wide to witness the entertainment on display. It was a very different lifestyle than what the Arabs were used to.

As Muhammad led the caravan to the marketplace, he noticed the armoured guards standing by its entrance, equipped with spears and shields. At first glance, they made for an unwelcoming appearance, but they warmly greeted the Arab merchants who they were familiar with after years of reliable trade. The smell of frankincense and spices drifting over from the stalls intrigued them as they were shown to the stables, where food and water awaited the animals. Excited but weary men unloaded the caravan, looking forward to the rest and food that the evening had in store.

The next day, Muhammad began to trade in the bustling marketplace. Although Maysara assumed the role of assistant, his attention was not only focused on business as he kept a close eye on Muhammad, whose behaviour continued to surprise him. Unlike most traders, not a single one of his transactions was earned by way of a lie or exaggeration. Honesty and transparency laced Muhammad's words and conduct. While the other Arab traders would swear oaths in the names of their idols to make people believe their claims, Maysara noticed that Muhammad never did this.

One afternoon, Muhammad decided to nap under a tree. Maysara rested nearby on a comfy chair, admiring the view and enjoying the break. Just then, a voice broke the peaceful silence.

"Praise the Lord!" yelled a short old man dressed in a thick, brown robe. A startled Maysara jumped up before realizing that it was only Nestor, the local monk from the Christian monastery nearby.

"Do my eyes deceive me, O Maysara?" the old man asked, the urgency in his small steps almost causing him to stumble over his robe. Nestor drew closer to Maysara, took a deep breath, and while pointing with his knobby finger, said, "Who is the man beneath the tree? What is his name?"

Maysara, taken aback, hesitated before answering. "He is Muhammad from the tribe of Hashim, the noblest of the Quraysh of Makkah."

"And tell me, boy, does he have a reddish glow in his eyes?" the monk asked while tugging on the silver cross around his neck.

Maysara thought for a moment before realizing that Muhammad's eyes did fit the description. "Praise the Lord!" the monk cheered when Maysara confirmed this and pulled him into an engulfing, tight hug. "Do you realize that none but the prophets have rested under that blessed tree? This is surely the future prophet foretold to us by Jesus."[9]

Maysara, trying his best not to look confused, forced a polite smile, but Nestor had already moved on to gaze admiringly at Muhammad as he lay there sound asleep. Although all this information made no sense to Maysara, something about it sounded true, in the certainty of Nestor's words as he expressed his wish to live long enough to witness the prophethood.

The confusion Maysara felt quickly disappeared as he recalled the two angelic clouds following Muhammad on their journey. There was certainly something different about Muhammad, and he was determined to share all these findings with Khadijah when they returned.

§

At long last, the caravan arrived in Makkah. Khadijah was surprised to find Maysara bursting through the courtyard, buzzing with excitement.

"Never before have we made such profits, my lady!" her loyal servant informed her. "Never before!" He then proceeded to plonk a big bag of gold and silver coins on the table. Khadijah's eyes widened. These were double what they usually earned!

"How?" was all she could ask.

Maysara then told her everything in vivid detail, starting with Muhammad's character and manners. Khadijah smiled in amazement as she listened. Hearing all the good things that Maysara had to say about Muhammad caused something to enter her heart; it was delicate and warm and felt a lot like hope. After many negative experiences in the past, she was thankful that she had finally found someone trustworthy to manage her business. Maysara did not neglect to mention the protective clouds or the claims of the monk. Not sure what to make of these details, Khadijah decided to consult her cousin Waraqa, a wise old man who had studied the scriptures of the Jews and Christians. Unlike the pagans of Makkah, he believed in only One Almighty Creator. He listened to her, deep in thought, until something clicked in his mind. His eyes lit up despite the blindness of old age clouding them. "Muhammad may very well be the long-awaited Prophet of God!"

Later that evening, Khadijah sat in contemplation, her room dimly lit by an oil lamp. Her mind and heart raced as she thought about the blessings in her life, the exceedingly fruitful trade, and the fact that Muhammad had expressed willingness to work for her again. She thought of his upright nature and kind demeanour, finding no doubt in her heart that he was a special person. Her trusted cousin's inclinations made her all the more sure of this. She found herself wondering if one such as Muhammad would be willing to marry her. She was now forty years of age and had been widowed twice, whereas he had not yet been married. She closed her eyes, thinking to herself. She would never know unless she asked…

A knock on the door interrupted her thoughts. Khadijah opened it to find her friend Nafisa standing there with a big smile strapped on her face, voicing a cheerful greeting.

They sat down amidst scattered cushions as they chatted. Nafisa sensed something was on Khadijah's mind. "What is on your mind, dear friend?" she asked. After some small talk Khadijah began to share her thoughts about Muhammad and then suggested the idea of marriage.

Nafisa, being a wise lady with an eye for matchmaking, immediately proclaimed that this was a great idea. She believed that Khadijah's character would complement Muhammad's quite nicely. "Leave it with me! Let me speak to Muhammad about this matter and convey your proposal."[10]

The next day, Nafisa hurried over to Abu Talib's house, where she was welcomed in by his family. When inside, there was no sign of any other men. Disappointed, she was hoping to find Muhammad nearby so that conversation would flow naturally. She asked to speak to Muhammad, and he was sent for promptly. After a few minutes, the anxious wait was over A handsome young man with dark hair complementing his full beard entered the room. His kind black eyes lowered in modesty as he greeted her.

"I've come to you on important business," she said before diving right in, asking if he would consider marriage. Before Muhammad could squeeze in a reply, she continued, "If a woman blessed with nobility, beauty, and wealth wanted to marry you, would you be interested?" Nafisa hinted. Surprised, Muhammad scanned his mind to think who that person could be.

Who would even consider me for marriage knowing that I am an orphan? I neither have a decent job nor my own place to live. These thoughts crossed his mind, so he expressed his concerns. Nafisa waved away his worries. Wearing a knowing smile, she assured him that those were not at all deterrents for the lady who was interested in him.

"And who is she?" he finally asked, curiosity growing.

He appeared pleasantly surprised to learn that it was Khadijah. His fair complexion, slightly tanned by the sun, flushed a rosy pink out of shyness. Having formed a high opinion of Khadijah, he was honoured by this proposal. Nafisa noticed the surprise turn to happiness in Muhammad's face and could barely contain her delight, glad that the interest was now mutual. "Leave everything to me!" she assured him. And with that, the most beloved members of the tribe of Hashim and the tribe of Asad were joined in matrimony that was warmly welcomed and celebrated by the people.

Just as Nafisa suspected, Khadijah and Muhammad complemented each other beautifully; both excellent in manners and generous in the community. On her visits, she would notice the brightness of Khadijah's face, the flow of true, unrequited love lighting up her eyes. When she happened to witness their interactions, the couple's dynamic was one of mutual respect and sincerity. There was never a time when Muhammad entered the home that the two would not exchange heartfelt greetings with such eagerness as though becoming acquainted for the first time.

In the many happy years that passed, Khadijah and Muhammad were blessed with six beautiful children, two boys: Qasim and Abdullah, and four girls: Zaynab, Ruqayya, Umm Kulthum, and Fatimah. Tragedy struck when each boy passed away in their infancy, leaving behind a heartbroken family. Khadijah and Muhammad helped each other through their grief with the hope that one day they would be reunited with their sons in the Afterlife. That their family would all be together once more, whole and complete. Nonetheless, both strove to make their home a wholesome one filled with love, warmth, and togetherness. Despite not having his father around, fatherhood came naturally to Muhammad. He was the best to their children, earning the affection of even Khadijah's young servant, Zayd, who became like a son to him. When Khadijah heard that despite being freed, Zayd still favoured their household, her heart swelled with happiness. No visitor nor servant nor person in need felt like a stranger in their household. This was one of the many values that they shared.

Khadijah was more than only a wife or the mother of his children. To Muhammad, she was his dearest friend who shared his ideals about the world and belief in the one true God, Allah. Their loving marriage increased Muhammad's reputation and honour in society until many among the tribe of Hashim thought that he would soon take up the position of chief and follow in the footsteps of his late grandfather, Abdul Muttalib. However, Muhammad was not concerned with such matters and showed little interest in public affairs.

When Muhammad was forty years old, he started noticing many strange occurrences in his life. For some time now, he had been telling his wife about the vivid dreams he kept experiencing. In these dreams, he would see the events of the next day in startling detail, and sure enough, the next day, he found that they turned out to be true. Each time these incidents unfolded, it left him astonished. He wondered what such dreams were pointing him to. These true dreams caused Muhammad to feel a strong desire to seek solitude, keeping away from the company of people.

He began to spend time alone in one of the caves on the outskirts of Makkah.[11] His wife and children sensed this change and supported his retreats away from home. During these trips, it often happened that after he had left the town and was approaching the mountainous areas, he would clearly hear the words: "Peace be on thee, O Messenger of God." He would turn to look for the speaker, only to find no one in sight. It was as if the words had come from a tree or a stone.

When the month of Ramadan arrived, Khadijah prepared some supplies and, with a tight embrace, she bid him farewell as he left for his retreat. Leaning up against the door, she watched the back of her husband until he was nothing more than a silhouette, soon vanishing from her gaze. Muhammad had discovered the Cave of Hira, a completely remote space in the weathered rock, about an hour's walk from his home. To reach it, he had to climb a small mountain and manoeuvre to the other side of a second small peak. Following a narrow path soon revealed the entrance to the secluded cave.

The cave was so small that it would have been difficult for even two people to be there together. Muhammad liked to sit in its entrance, on the edge of the mountain, overlooking the whole of Makkah. From here, he could see the Ka'bah far below. At a greater distance away, the barren desert stretched out almost infinitely, cloaked in empty darkness. His eyes would shift from looking at the glorious Ka'bah, the house of Allah, to the stone idols and entertainers that surrounded it. Though the sounds of pagan chants, prayers, and mystical music were too far away to reach him, it still filled him with unease. The troubling thoughts that first arose during his days as a boy, while sitting in the shade of the Ka'bah with Abdul Muttalib, had rekindled. These concerns had been quietly rising in significance and were now weighing him down like a heavy stone. Inside the cave, he would spend his time worshipping Allah and pondering over life.

Away from other people, with only nature as his company, Muhammad searched for peace and meaning. He had never taken part in idol worship, had not shared many of the values of the region's tribes, and had kept his distance from superstition and injustices. However, Muhammad loved his people and desired a bright future for them, a future of peace, justice and true faith in Allah. In the comforting confines of the cave, he sat in silence, eyes closed and heart searching. This spiritual quest naturally led him towards the calling that many small signs had been pointing to throughout his life.

It was during the month of Ramadan in the year 610 that this lifelong quest for answers, the gradual build-up of blessings and adversities, would reach a defining point on the lonely summit of the mountain. Here, guidance would descend upon Muhammad with crushing power and definitive direction, and though his questions would be answered, he would be ushered into a new stage. Life for Muhammad would change very drastically. Though the change would bring with it clarity and purpose, his world would be turned upside down, marking the start of a life of struggle and sacrifice.

Chapter 5
Shock & Awe

Soft, silvery moonlight illuminated the lofty mountains, casting a cool hue upon the lonely summit that hosted Muhammad's contemplative retreats. These mountains overlooking Makkah bore witness to many occurrences since the beginning of creation. They stood tall, ever-vigilant, since the dawn of man till the historic day when Abraham left his wife and son in what was once an empty desert but would later become a hub of trade and pilgrims. This particular area served as the backdrop for many historical stories, though none as momentous as the incident that unfolded one tranquil night.

Monday, 10 August 610 | Ramadan

Alone in the Cave of Hira, Muhammad spent his time supplicating to Allah, engaged in sincere prayer. Heart uneasy and soul yearning, he longed to worship his Creator as He would want to be worshipped, like his forefather Prophet Abraham had done. Over his shoulder, Makkah appeared thickly wrapped in the evening's silence. A few glimmers of firelight dotted various households in the far distance. A blanket of stars burned brightly from above, outshining the dim lights in the city below. It was a sight to be admired, a view one could only truly appreciate from afar. To sit back and take in the scenery, one could easily become engrossed, melting into the shadows of the night, unaware of the passing of time until dawn awakened. However, prayer and contemplation occupied Muhammad's time, filling his mind and keeping him grounded so that he did not get swept away by the enchantment of the evening. In this place of refuge, he appreciated the solitude and the peace that came with it. Muhammad sat in the confines of the cave, eyes resting shut for a brief moment until something pulled him into focus. His eyes snapped open as he sensed the presence of someone else.

As he turned around, a figure appeared in the corner of his eye so suddenly and silently that he thought it had come out of thin air. Muhammad could barely react. Before he could say a single word, the figure ordered him: "Read!"

Unbeknown to Muhammad, this was the Archangel Jibril in the form of a man. Hearing this voice echoing off the wall startled him, as he had not heard anyone approaching. Being unlettered, unable to read or write like most of the people of Makkah, Muhammad felt he could not comply with this puzzling demand.

"I am not of those who can read!" he replied.

Without any warning, the angel embraced him, squeezing him so tightly that Muhammad thought he would surely lose consciousness. Just as he thought he would pass out, he was released, only to once again hear the command: "Read!"

The demand bounced off the shadowed walls of the small cave, filling it entirely. The presence, the voice, the suddenness of it all rang many bells, summoning memories from the recesses of his childhood when he encountered the two figures who opened his chest. Muhammad stood there stunned and confused. He could only muster up enough energy to repeat his first reply, this time saying it as more of a plea.

"I am not of those who can read."

Then, the angel overwhelmed him again with a tight embrace, holding it until Muhammad could not take any more. He gasped for air and was then released.

"Read!" came the impossible command once more. When Muhammad gave the same reply again, the angel gave him one final powerful squeeze, before releasing him.[12] This time the being said:

> *"Read, O Prophet in the Name of your Lord Who created– created humans from a clinging substance. Read! And your Lord is the Most Generous, Who taught by the pen- taught man what he never knew."*
>
> [Qur'an 96: 1–5]

The words shook Muhammad to his core. His heart pounded so loudly he could hear it. He did not know how to make sense of what was happening. His mind and heart racing with frightening intensity, he did not even notice when and how the figure left the cave. One thing, however, was very clear. Those words had pierced through all the fright, becoming firmly etched onto his heart. He could still hear them ringing in his ears. They were, in fact, the words of Allah that He had chosen to reveal to Muhammad on that night, simultaneously elevating him to the position of a Prophet of God. From that moment onwards, the chapter of Muhammad's life as an ordinary man came to an end. He was now the Chosen One.

He did not realize this, however. The dizziness of a thousand thoughts swirled around in his mind all at once. *Have I been possessed by an evil spirit? Perhaps I've lost my mind? Who or what was that?[13]*

All he wanted to do was leave and return home. He stumbled out of the cave in a state of shock and readied himself to climb down the mountain.

He had barely moved a foot when he heard the voice calling out from above, seemingly coming from every direction, surrounding him. His feeling of confusion turned into stone-cold dread and when Muhammad looked up, his eyes widened at what he saw.

"Muhammad! You are now the Messenger of Allah and I am the angel Jibril!" the angel announced.[14] He was now clearly visible as a man, levitating in the sky.

Muhammad froze, his eyes fixed on the otherworldly man that was calling himself the angel Jibril. He knew without a doubt that this claim could only be the truth—this was indeed an angel. When the angel began to move upwards, Muhammad fled down the mountain. He could hear the words being repeated in the distance but dared not turn to look again. Instead, he headed straight home as quickly as his feet could carry him.

"Cover me! Cover me!" he said to Khadijah as soon as she opened the door. She reached out her hand to help steady him as he entered their house. His face was ashen, paler than the moon outside, and he appeared disorientated. Alarmed, she quickly brought a cloak and gently placed it over his shivering body. Not wanting to add to his distress, she sat beside him, waiting for her husband to calm.

With his heart still hammering inside his chest, he laid down on the rug. The only light was the flickering flame in the oil lamp across the room. The children were all fast asleep and the house was calm, completely undisturbed as though it was just another night. Except there was nothing at all regular about that evening. Khadijah could tell that something drastic had happened. She checked her husband's forehead. It was cool to the touch.

Muhammad looked at his wife. "Khadijah, I don't know what's happened to me," he said, voice weary as he lay with his hand over his forehead.

Khadijah placed his hand underneath the cloak, soothing him, and patiently waiting for him to gather his thoughts. Being a wise and considerate woman, she wanted him to speak at his own pace without pressuring him with any questions that may add to his distress. Eventually, his body stopped shivering and the shock subsided. Sensing this, she finally asked him what the matter was.

Muhammad explained what took place in the cave that night. He described the heavenly being, the crushing experience, the instructions that were given so firmly, and the extraordinary words revealed to him—five verses that had been permanently imprinted on his heart. When he finished describing his experience, he sat up and firmly looked his beloved wife in her eyes. "I am truly scared for myself," he admitted.

Khadijah recognized the urgency of the moment. Driven by the need to support her husband, she shared some of the most powerful words spoken in her life.

"No," she said. She held his hands in hers tightly. "I don't believe that. I don't believe Allah would want that. He would never do that to a man like you." She held him close. "He wouldn't lower you like that." She leaned forward, shaking her head reassuringly. "You are kind to your family, take care of the poor and needy, honour your guests, and you support those in difficulty."[15]

The confidence with which she spoke lifted her husband's spirits and her faith brought comfort to his heart. Muhammad began to wonder: *Could I really be a Prophet of God now? What is it that God wants from me?*

He couldn't put a finger on what it all meant.

On the other hand, as Khadijah pondered over her husband's words, her mind began to connect various instances in their life until she was left with strong certainty. Allah would never disgrace or abandon one as sincere and pious as her husband. Whatever happened in that cave was a sign of something tremendous. She felt that, perhaps, Allah had indeed chosen Muhammad just as Nestor the monk had suggested to her servant Maysara all those many years ago during the caravan trip to Bosra.

When the morning sun had fully risen, they headed to the house of Waraqa, who Khadijah hoped could provide some insight about the whole incident. "My dearest cousin Khadijah! It has been too long." Waraqa greeted, welcoming them in as they announced their presence.

His modest home was nearly overcrowded by scrolls stacked against the walls and scattered across a solitary wooden table. Thick sheets were knocked into the dusty beige wall, covered with scores of unfamiliar script. The writing was indecipherable, but the smell of ink hung fresh. Although his eyes were glazed over, Waraqa turned his head, his gaze seemingly following the two as they took their seat upon a taut leather cushion. The loss of his eyesight, due to years of studying and old age, only served to strengthen his sense of intuition. Although Waraqa could no longer read any writing, he remained an expert in reading the mood.

Waraqa could sense that something immense had happened to his visitors even as they sat down.

Khadijah wasted no time to approach her cousin with the weight of what had happened; there was no other learned person in Makkah that she respected nor trusted as much. "O my cousin, please listen to your nephew!" she implored, referring to Muhammad, who through marriage was now considered a close relative to their tribe.

"What have you seen, my nephew?" Waraqa asked him, tilting his head as he listened attentively.

Muhammad recalled the events of the night before. Waraqa's bristly white eyebrows arched upwards. He leaned forward in amazement, his chair slightly buckling beneath him. "This is the same angel that Allah sent to Moses!" he exclaimed to their surprise.

At this, Muhammad looked down, his mind concluding that this could only mean one thing. The words that were revealed to him, his experience, therefore, meant that...

"You too must be chosen like him to be God's Messenger!" Waraqa explained, giving voice to Muhammad's thoughts. Excited, the old man extended his hand forward to feel out Muhammad's forehead and then leaned over to kiss it. "I wish I were young so that I could live to see the day your people will drive you out of this city," he sighed, his forehead creased in worry.

Muhammad and Khadijah exchanged worried glances.

"Will they drive me out of my own home?" Muhammad asked, uncertainly.

The shocking nature of the prediction seemed too far-fetched to believe as the people of Makkah had no quarrels with him, in fact, they admired and loved him. Furthermore, it seemed unlikely that the Quraysh would disown him, the grandson of the great Abdul Muttalib they all revered and honoured. The loyalty between families and tribes was almost unbreakable—driving anyone out of their land was an impossible notion.

Yet Waraqa did not find this unlikely at all. The old man nodded solemnly. "Most certainly," he replied with great seriousness. "Never has someone come with a message like the one you will deliver, except that his people will turn against him. They will call you a liar, abuse you, and may even banish you. And should I live to see the day, I will stand by you and support your cause!" [16]

Waraqa's foreboding prediction was met with stunned silence. The weight of realization began to set in. Muhammad was no longer just Muhammad the tradesman or Muhammad of the Hashim Tribe, but he was now Muhammad the Messenger of Allah.

Khadijah looked at her husband with his dark eyes fixed ahead, eyebrows drawn close together in deep thought. Coming to terms with this new identity was a daunting effort, yet beneath the apprehension, a sense of purpose flickered to life within Muhammad. The two walked home with an undeniable understanding that life as they knew it would change for good. And true to Waraqa's words, what awaited was anything but easy.

Even though Muhammad had now officially become a Prophet and a leader, he had no idea that in a thousand years' time people all over the world would be pouring over the details of his life, hanging onto every letter of his sayings, and identifying themselves as a follower of his. Such is the power of Allah's decree. He plans out our lives in a manner we can never predict or calculate. We are all exactly where Allah intended us to be. No amount of questioning Allah's decree will change that. In fact, it may hurt us mentally and spiritually. Instead, we should ask ourselves: "How can I make the best of where Allah has placed me?" In all the years before becoming a Prophet, Muhammad had tried honestly to live in a way that a pure believer in Allah should—making the best of a bleak situation—and in return, Allah did not allow him to fail in his mission.

Chapter 6
Nearest & Dearest

As the initial shock from the incident subsided, the reassurances of Khadijah and Waraqa began to set in, and Muhammad felt ready to face the Cave of Hira once more.

The valley and sand-strewn tracks leading to the cave he knew so well from his time as a shepherd now felt eerie and foreign. And yet, the Prophet found himself often revisiting these remote parts in the days following the incident.[17] Staying at home only increased his restlessness, and so he sat crossed-legged, back straightened, enveloped by the mouth of the cave, hoping that Jibril would visit him again. Inhaling deeply, he cleared his mind of worldly thoughts. He knew that he had to prepare himself mentally and spiritually to be fully present should the moment arise. More than meeting Jibril again, he yearned to be touched by the Words of Allah, to experience the connection with the Divine.

One evening the Prophet hiked the steep pathway to the top of the mountain. He was close to the Cave of Hira when he heard a powerful voice calling his name. Startled, the Prophet looked around for a speaker. Seeing no one in front or behind him, he raised his head to look upwards. He stumbled back at what he saw—the Archangel Jibril, in his true angelic form.

Muhammad was in awe at the sight of the angel, seated upon a mighty throne that inconceivably seemed to occupy both the sky and earth. Jibril's 600 beautiful wings were encrusted with jewels, precious stones, and pearls that shimmered in splendour as they filled the horizon.[18] Overwhelmed, the Prophet fell to his knees, his heart racing just like the last time, if not more. Confusion and terror overcame him, the sight too overwhelming to behold.

Just then, Jibril's majestic voice pierced the air. "O Muhammad, *you* are without doubt the Messenger of Allah." His tone was reassuring.

The cold grip of fright began to fade from the Prophet's heart, replaced with a soft wave of hope and conviction. Nonetheless, the incident left him shaken to the core. "Khadijah, Khadijah, pour cold water over my head," the Prophet said breathlessly as soon as he staggered into the house.

Khadijah knew straight away that her husband must have encountered the angel again. As the Prophet sat on the ground still trying to catch his breath, she brought over a pail of water. Gently, she scooped over some handfuls onto his head. She could feel heat radiate from his hair even before she touched him.

"Please wrap me up in a blanket," he requested.

Once again, Khadijah covered her husband. She sat beside him, her presence a calming support. The Prophet drew the blanket tightly over his shoulders, the fabric bunched in his slightly tremoring hand. Wrapped up, he stared at the ceiling.

"On the horizon, I saw the same angel who had come to me in the Cave of Hira," he finally spoke, his voice steady.

Khadijah listened attentively as he went into detail about his astonishing experience. Midway through the conversation, she noticed a faraway look appearing in his eyes, which slowly closed as if slipping into a trance. Beads of sweat formed on his forehead then trickled down, disappearing into his thick beard. Khadijah inched closer, hand raised slightly, uncertain if her touch would shock him.

After a short pause, his eyes reopened and he bolted up, the blanket dropping off his shoulders. His heart fluttered with the weight of the new Revelation received from the Heavens. He immediately began to articulate it in the form of a melodious recital:

> *"You, wrapped in your cloak! Stand up and warn. Revere your Lord alone. Purify your garments. Continue to shun idols. Do not do a favour expecting more in return. be steadfast for the sake of your Lord."*
>
> **[Qur'an 74: 1–6]**

The message was loud and clear. Now, as a Messenger of Allah, he could not keep what he knew to himself.

"What are you to do, O Muhammad?" Khadijah asked in amazement.

Muhammad sat down again as he pondered the profound words imprinted in his heart. "To worship Allah as One and to share this news with our people," he answered.

He wondered how he would go about this mission. How could he share the Message when what he had to say would be considered outrageous by most of society?

As if she could read his mind, Khadijah said, "The people follow the beliefs of their parents and grandparents with the fiercest loyalty."

The Prophet nodded, expression serious. He knew very well the depth of his people's attachment to the idols and the wealth that would be at stake should he ask them to abandon their beliefs.

How could Laat, Manaat or Hubal be false gods? They would protest. It would mean their grandparents and forefathers were misguided—a thought that was too despicable for them to entertain. They would surely object.

The Prophet thought long and hard about this. He decided to first reach out to those closest to him. Besides Khadijah and Waraqa, all his daughters, as well as young Ali, and Zayd were the first to embrace his message. The members of his household were amongst his nearest and dearest. With full confidence, they readily accepted what he brought, knowing him to be truthful and sincere.

Next was Abu Bakr, Muhammad's best friend since the age of fifteen. Abu Bakr was a slender man of fair complexion who was two years younger than him. A wealthy businessman, he was known for his honesty and good character. The Prophet hastened to see his friend soon after the second Revelation. Steam rose gently from the auburn-coloured tea which rested atop the serving tray. A bowl of dates was presented to him. Sitting across from his dear friend, the Prophet wasted no time with small talk and cut straight to the chase.

Abu Bakr, being from the elite, had a lot to lose, which is why the Prophet did not know how he would react. His friend listened silently at the description of the angel. The message to worship one God made perfect sense to him. So little remained of the teachings of Abraham and Jesus, and Arabia was saturated with idolatry and injustice. When Muhammad recited the verses that were revealed to him, they seized Abu Bakr's heart. He knew without a doubt that those were the words of the Creator; no poem nor story had the same far-reaching effects on the soul.

Without hesitation, Abu Bakr reached out to grasp his friend's hand.

"I swear by my father and mother that you have never lied and would never say anything about God that is untrue," he declared, and to the Prophet's pleasant surprise, went on to say, "Therefore, there is none worthy of worship than God, and you are the Messenger of God."

And with that, Abu Bakr became the first man to embrace Islam; Khadijah being the first woman, and Ali the first youth. In this way, the Prophet Muhammad cultivated a group of loyal supporters from among his close family and friends. With the support of Abu Bakr, the circle of early Muslims grew slowly but surely.

Khadijah smiled to herself, grateful that her husband's mission progressed, that other hearts would be free from the shackles of servitude to idols and material things. After embracing this pure faith, life felt steeped in blessings and meaning. The inner peace was unmatched.

"Has Ali returned yet?" she asked softly as she entered the room.

The Prophet nodded. "He waits outside with Zayd."

Whenever possible, the Prophet held private gatherings with his followers. To avoid the suspicion of their neighbours, the venue often rotated. The two youths had been responsible for conveying news of the arrangement to the others.

"We will leave shortly before *qayloolah*," he said, referring to the midday nap. During this time, the streets would be relatively empty as most people retreated to relax in their homes, seeking shelter from the noontime heat.

With a warm smile, he greeted his wife and bent down to kiss their sleeping daughter. Their youngest, Fatimah, had not been feeling well and was curled up on the woollen rug nearby. Khadijah watched as Muhammad, Ali, and Zayd, three figures of various heights, made their way out of the neighbourhood. She looked forward to when their home would once again be blessed to host the next gathering.

Usually, the small group of Muslims arranged to meet at whichever home was offered. During quiet times, they walked the streets in groups of two. The more cautious, whose lofty families would not at all be pleased with them, arrived at their destination one at a time, striving to remain unnoticed.

Other times, the early Muslims would gather outside Makkah near the hills, listening to the recitation of Revelation—the glorious Qur'an, as the Prophet called it. The verses uplifted the desolate area, the captivating words penetrating their hearts. Prophet Muhammad, standing on a slightly raised outcrop, would face his followers and teach them everything he had been instructed. He spoke of what it really meant to worship their Creator without associating any partner or equals with him. He spoke passionately about the rights of the oppressed like the orphans and the poor.

Bilal, a black Abyssinian slave, was a secret believer who snatched every opportunity to be in the company of Muhammad. Sitting amidst the assembly of tribespeople and servants, he listened as the Prophet, unassuming and humble, addressed them with the sincerity of someone who truly cared about their wellbeing. Muhammad was dressed in a simple white robe, absent of any extravagance Bilal expected from a leader, being accustomed to the silken garments and jewelled rings that his master flaunted.

Bilal looked at the others in the gathering, noticing the tranquillity on their faces—they hung onto every word being preached. Some eyes welled with tears and others glimmered with raging determination as Muhammad called for social justice, fairness, and peace. In these gatherings, Bilal's heart soared free.

Prophet Muhammad raised his hand and said to them, "I shall be in Paradise like this," he held his two fingers together, "next to the one who supports an orphan."

As well as teaching his followers these values, he also taught them how to offer prayer and perform a religiously prescribed wash called *wudu* that would prepare them for prayer. The group had gathered at noon and before they knew it, time had made way for orange hues to stretch forth in the sky. The people dispersed, hearts hopeful, and souls rejuvenated as they looked forward to their next gathering.

However, despite the support of his gradually growing circle, the Prophet became uneasy. He had not seen or heard from Jibril since that second encounter. Many days had since passed, days turning to weeks, and weeks to months. The loneliness he felt made it seem as though a lifetime had elapsed. Khadijah noticed his restlessness and they spoke at length about his concerns. The Prophet began to think that the pause in Revelation was because he had done something wrong or acted in a way that had angered Allah.

His longing and anticipation eventually morphed into deep-seated worry. Could it be that his Master had abandoned him? Eventually, the Revelation of a new chapter, Surah ad-Duha, freed him from all stress and doubt.

By the morning sunlight, and by the night when it grows still. Your Lord has not abandoned you, nor has He become hateful of you. And the next life is certainly far better for you than this one. And surely your Lord will give so much to you that you will be pleased. Did He not find you as an orphan then sheltered you? Did He not find you seeking then guided you? And did He not find you needy then satisfied your needs? So do not oppress the orphan, nor repulse the beggar. And proclaim the blessings of your Lord.

[Qur'an 93: 1–11]

The Prophet felt a calmness embrace his heart as the Revelation came to a close. The verses were a comfort from his Maker. Relieved that he had not been abandoned, he exhaled, eyes brimming with tears. Allah had been there for him all along! Hearing that Allah had planned a great future for him filled him with hope and excitement. The pause in Revelation, though distressing, instilled in him a greater sense of patience, humility, and appreciation for having a Divine connection.

Afterwards came other Revelations, gentler in tone. These confirmed and increased the reassurances already given to the Prophet. On one occasion, Jibril was in his presence, visible to him alone, as was normally the case. When Khadijah walked by, the angel said to him, "Give Khadijah the greetings of Peace from her Lord."

Muhammad called to her, "O Khadijah!" She paused in her step, momentarily surprised. Her husband smiled as he spoke. "Here is Jibril who wishes to greet you with the greeting of Peace from your Lord."

Khadijah's heart leapt, deeply moved by this acknowledgement. When she could find the words to speak, she answered, "Allah is Peace, and from Him is Peace, and on Jibril be Peace!"[19]

A distance away from these developments was a man by the name of Amr who was searching for the truth. He lived in a small town miles away from Makkah. For a long time, feelings of anger and irritation had been building up inside of him. The pagan traditions of his people just felt wrong.

How can I worship idols that can't benefit or harm me? He wondered.

One day, he decided to leave his home city. With nothing but his sword and a burlap sack filled with a few days' provisions, he went searching across the Arabian deserts for someone who shared his concerns. Someone who also longed to worship the one true Creator. Every time he entered a new city, he would ask the people, "Is there anyone amongst you bringing some news or saying anything out of the ordinary?"

Amr was met with disappointing replies. Nearing the end of his limit, he rode off in the desert and decided to sit under a tree for shade. Squinting, he noticed a rider coming forward in the distance. Amr waved at him. Soon, the camel hobbled closer and a young man hopped off. He straightened his tunic before greeting the middle-aged man with a respectful nod.

"Where are you from?" Amr asked him.

"From Makkah, the home of the Ka'bah," replied the rider.

Amr's eyebrows perked up with curiosity. "Come sit," he invited. Noticing the man eyeing his leather pouch, he offered him some water. The rider made himself comfortable, resting his back against the strong tree trunk as he bemoaned the heat of the sun.

Amr remained silent, merely watching the man quench his thirst. He then leaned forward with the same question he had asked countless others.

"Do you have any news to share?" He knew that Makkah was the hub of idol worship, yet still, he questioned, "Is there anyone amongst you bringing some news or saying anything out of the ordinary?"

Expecting to hear the usual response, he was surprised when the man said, "Yes. There is, in fact, a man with a strange message."

Amr's eyes widened. He gestured for the man to speak further. The rider shrugged. "All I will say is this: he doesn't care much for our gods."

Amr tried to hide his smile to no avail. "That is exactly the man I am looking for!" he exclaimed, unable to contain his eagerness.

Quickly, he snatched his leather pouch and jumped onto his horse, heading in the direction of Makkah. When he arrived, he went straight to the Ka'bah. The stench of sacrifices from hours ago caused him to grit his teeth as he passed the popular idol pedestals. Since this was where most people would gather, he began making enquiries. No one quite knew how to respond to him.

"Have you heard of the message?" he asked a young woman. She blinked at him, perplexed. A stout, yellow-clad man, presumably her superior, beckoned to her and she scurried off to polish one of the idols. After much effort, Amr realized that the man he was seeking must have been operating in private. Surely no one in this den of idols would know what he was referring to.

Unhappy, he walked away as the din of chanting and chatter faded in the background. "He must not want to draw attention to himself or those who follow him," he mused as he turned into the residential area nearby.

Two-story homes stood adjacent from each other, casting shadows over the sloping path. Amr looked left and right for anyone who fit the image conjured by his mind. Eventually, after some asking around, his enquiries led him to the door of Khadijah. He was invited inside by a young, bright-eyed boy with curly hair. A few members of the household welcomed him. At long last, he found himself in the company of the man he sought.

Despite Amr being a complete stranger, Muhammad received him warmly, willing to hear him out. After a brief exchange of greetings, Amr's tone became serious. He looked pointedly at the dark-haired man before him and asked, "Who exactly are you?"

Muhammad simply replied, "I am a Prophet."

Amr had absolutely no idea what that meant, so he probed, "And what is a Prophet?"

"It is someone who Allah sends with a message."

"And what is this message you have been given?"

"That we should all take care of our families, do away with the idols, and worship Allah, the one true God who has no partners or equals," Muhammad explained.

Although concise, it was a lot of information for Amr to digest. Reading between the lines, he realized that adopting this message would mean becoming part of a life-changing mission. "And who has chosen to join you in this mission?" Amr dug further.

The Prophet had only just met Amr and had already told him all he needed to know. Any further information would place his small band of followers in harm's way, for already whispers had begun to spread amongst the people of a belief at odds with the traditions. "A free person and a slave," was all he said, an indirect reference to Abu Bakr and Bilal.

Amr understood the sensitive nature of his question and did not probe further. He straightened his posture, eyes shining with determination. "I too wish to be of your followers! And to declare that in public!"

The Prophet lightly waved his hand as if to calm Amr down. "You cannot do that right now," he cautioned. "Did you not see the delicate situation I am in and the nature of my people?"

Amr nodded in understanding. What the Prophet said next stunned him. "However, what you should do is return to your family and when news reaches you of my victory, then come to me."

And so, Amr returned home with a renewed sense of purpose and a belief to impart to his family. He was now a Companion of the Prophet, and one of the earliest people to accept Islam. He sat on this prediction of a future victory for many years, waiting for the day to meet the Prophet again, hoping that he would be remembered.[20]

Whether a neighbour or a traveller from the outskirts of Makkah, the Prophet's followers increased in number as time went by. When free from the presence of hostile disbelievers, the Muslims greeted each other with the words given to the Prophet by Jibril as the greeting of the people of Paradise, "*As-salaamu 'alaykum!* Peace be on you." To which the answer was "And on you be Peace!"

A weary huntsman stood behind an affluent merchant, both customers of a bread maker who diligently arranged an assortment of barley bread. The three shared this greeting discreetly, enjoying a moment of quiet companionship as they stood in the throngs of a marketplace lively with upcoming festivities. In a narrow alleyway not too far away, a noblewoman with an exquisite trailing cloak crossed paths with a young servant girl and returned the greeting given to her. Cutting through trade and class, these words between the early Muslims had the instantaneous power to fill their hearts with serenity and an increasing throb of determination. They were Believers and they were in this together.

The message of Islam resonates with the souls of humanity. The desire to worship the one who created you with a direct connection is part of human nature, and this is why people such as Amr were already gravitating towards this idea even before the Prophet began his mission. The light of Revelation only adds to this internal desire to worship the Creator and provides it with direction in order to fulfil that desire and protect it from being corrupted by false ideas and beliefs.

Chapter 7
Don't Be Idle

The first three years of prophethood flew by with relative ease. Prophet Muhammad reached out privately to his family members and anyone else who he could trust—he sensed that the time was not yet right to go public.

Ali was only a child when the Prophet's mission began. Though technically his older cousin, Muhammad was more like a second father to the boy. Ali had been living under his guardianship ever since his father, Abu Talib, was unable to provide for all his children. During these three years, he accepted Islam at the tender age of ten, making him the first child to embrace the faith. As for Abu Talib, he made no objection to Ali nor his other son, Ja'far, for accepting Islam. Despite this, it was hugely disappointing for Muhammad to find his dearest uncle unwilling to forsake the religion of his forefathers.

Abu Talib felt a strong allegiance to his people, and the respect he had for his late father prevented him from turning his back on their ways. *After all, what would people say if the son of Abdul Muttalib abandoned his tradition?* Abu Talib would tell himself every time the Prophet would lovingly extend the invite to accept his message. Graciously, he would listen, but he remained silent.

As for the Prophet's other uncles, Abbas was evasive and Hamza was reluctant to hear him out, though both assured him of their unfailing affection for him personally. Abu Lahab, on the other hand, showed plainly his conviction that his nephew was delusional or perhaps even out to deceive others. Although the Prophet had not yet preached his message in public, the Quraysh caught wind of the news each time someone particularly significant was rumoured to have joined him. Bit by bit, the people began finding his increasingly growing circle of followers uncomfortable and annoying—especially the tribal chiefs.

§

A large reddish house built with solid clay bricks boasted immaculate arched windows that overlooked the Ka'bah. This place was known as Darun Nadwah—the equivalent of a Town Hall, but reserved only for the elite. Here, the tribal leaders would gather to discuss important matters.

One evening, the main room, as spacious as a cavern, hosted a few brightly burning oil lanterns. The flickering glow eerily lit up the large table around which everyone gathered. The meeting was in full swing. Sitting at the head of the creaky table were Walid, Abu Sufyan and Utbah—the leaders of three powerful tribes in Makkah. The Prophet's uncles Abu Lahab and Abu Talib were also present, watching the restless pacing of Abu Jahl. Up and down the room, the sleek yet robust tribesman walked with a glass of wine balanced between his fingers while the extravagantly dressed Walid rattled off the main issues to discuss.

"But before we begin, can I ask, what has happened to Abu Bakr?" Abu Jahl interrupted, though he knew the answer. "It has been quite some time since we last saw his face at our meetings."

Abu Sufyan, the youngest of the group, casually waved a hand. "He must be occupied with his business, I assume," he said as his mind, once again, wandered to his work.

"Yes, *business*..." Abu Jahl all but rolled his eyes.

As a prominent merchant in charge of Makkah's major trading operations, it appeared that Abu Sufyan had been too busy to notice that Abu Bakr was a Muslim for three years now. This was quite baffling to Abu Jahl, for Abu Bakr had no qualms about showing it.

Shaybah absentmindedly fidgeted with the jewelled rings decorating his thick fingers. "Speaking of absence, what of your nephew?" he asked, glancing at the uncles of Muhammad.

"Indeed, we do not see *him* here with us either," Abu Jahl chimed in, gesturing with his now-empty glass squarely in the face of Abu Lahab, not in the least bothered that this was his senior.

At this, the elderly man rose slowly into an upright position. He leaned forward, the table groaning beneath his weight as he responded, "Well, what can I say about my nephew except that I had high hopes in him."

At that moment, Abu Talib, although sitting in the gathering, felt that he would've much rather been elsewhere. His intense love for Muhammad created an instinctive response when he heard the slightest criticism of his nephew. "Muhammad is a good man," he said to the assembly in such a way that there was no room for argument.

The men nodded in general agreement, trying to ease the tension.

Then, with a pointed look, Abu Talib turned to his brother. "I see the wisdom of our father Abdul Muttalib in him. You do remember what father would say about him, *don't you*?" He fired back at Abu Lahab with an intimidating gaze.

Abu Lahab merely shrugged.

"Though he has always been distant from our ways," Abu Jahl remarked.

Walid stood up to join Abu Jahl in the middle of the room, his luxurious striped robe trailing behind him. The golden necklace hanging around his neck glistened. "Abu Jahl is correct," he agreed. "This has become increasingly obvious to us in recent times…"

Encouraged by this, Abu Jahl then swiftly moved across the room, placing his glass down. He pressed his fists on the table, leaning towards Abu Talib. "The activities of your nephew concerns me. You know he thinks ill of our gods and yet you do nothing!"

Utbah, one of the wealthiest of the Quraysh, had been listening quietly all along, resting his sagging cheeks in both hands. His narrow, tired eyes added to his overall sullen appearance. Finally, he piped in, "We've spoken to you about this before and you said you would take care of it." His chest puffed out a little as he referred to the previous meetings in which this issue was raised. When he was done saying his piece, he exchanged glances with Abu Jahl as if to hand over a baton.

"I see you've all been scheming behind my back," said Abu Talib as he stood up abruptly to leave. "My nephew has never insulted the gods nor does he speak openly about his ideas."

"And when he does speak openly? What then will you do, O Abu Talib?" pushed Walid, raising a crooked eyebrow.

The question was met with silence. Abu Talib left feeling torn inside. What could he have possibly answered? He loved Muhammad like a son but what he was preaching was clearly at odds with the ways of the Arabs, and more importantly, their forefathers. Little did Abu Talib know that it would not be too long before he would have to confront this dilemma and pick a side.

One night, the Prophet received Revelation commanding him to take his mission to the next stage.[21]

> So by your Lord! We will certainly question them all about what they used to do. So proclaim what you have been commanded, and turn away from the polytheists.
>
> [Qur'an 15: 92–94]

The instruction struck like lightning and Muhammad shot up, hastening out of the room. He called for Ali. After a moment, the young boy appeared from around the corner, curious wide eyes fixed on Muhammad. The Prophet then told him, "Allah has commanded me to warn my whole tribe now and the task will require all the help I can get. Prepare a feast with a leg of mutton and a jug of milk and invite them all over. I plan on telling them what I have been commanded to say."

Up until this point, the Prophet had only spoken to family members he could trust. Those he thought would react badly to his message were many, but now they all had to be spoken to, and the Prophet felt the pressure of the impending encounter. Anything could happen. The situation was volatile.

Ali followed the instructions to the letter using the Prophet's limited wealth to the best of his abilities. The following evening about forty people arrived at the house expecting nothing more than milk, mutton, and good company. The men filled the room, looking forward to filling their stomachs as they made their way to the cushions lining the wall. As the guests took their seats, the Prophet signalled to Ali for the food to be brought out. Then, he took a piece of meat, tore off a shred, and took one bite, placing the remainder back into the pot.

"Everyone, please eat in the name of Allah," he announced.

The guests were more than happy to oblige. They ate in relays, several at a time, until not one of them could eat any more. Ali was sitting nearby. He looked on in amazement at the satisfied guests and then at the pot of food. Even though each person took a full portion from the pot, he saw no change in the amount. It was as if people were simply stirring the pot and not taking anything out.

By Allah, if this pot was served to just one man, he could have eaten all of it! The young boy was alarmed at the bottomless quality of the seemingly small pot. He stared on in wonderment before noticing the Prophet beckoning him.

"Give them something to drink," he instructed Ali.

The young boy brought out the jug and poured each person a glass. Again, each person drank their fill, though one man alone could have emptied that jug. When the Prophet sensed the moment was right, he readied himself to make a speech. He began to rise when someone let out a throaty cough. Abu Lahab, who had been suspecting something to unfold at the dinner the moment he received the invite, interrupted the Prophet before he could begin. "I must take my leave," he announced, pushing his emptied plate aside before making his abrupt exit. A few men followed behind, and soon enough, the guests stood up, ready to take their leave. The opportunity was lost.

As the Prophet watched them go, the words of Allah rang in his ears: "*So proclaim what you have been commanded and turn away from the polytheists.*" He could not simply give up then and there.

The next day, he asked Ali to do exactly as he had done the previous day. Another meal was prepared, and everything went as before, except this time the Prophet waited for an opportunity during the meal to make his speech. The guests enjoyed the food, scooping flavourful barley with their fingers and laughing heartily at the tales told by the wittiest of their fellow tribesmen. As soon as there was a lull in the conversation, the Prophet grasped the moment.

"I celebrate Allah's praise, I seek His help, I believe in Him, I put my trust in Him, and bear witness that there is no God to be worshipped but Allah with no partners." As he paused to take a breath, the Prophet noticed some men exchange looks across the room. They rolled their eyes as if to say: *see how Muhammad conveniently forgets to mention the names of Laat, Manaat, and Hubal—typical!*

Still, he remained steadfast. "O sons of Abdul Muttalib," the Prophet continued, and the crowd felt the passion in his voice fill the room. "I know of no Arab who has come to his people with a nobler message than mine. I come to you bearing a message that will give the best of this world and the next."

Some faces appeared confused, their foreheads creasing, resembling the folds in their tightly-wrapped turbans. *Was there really another life after death?* They wondered, the notion utterly foreign to them.

With complete sincerity, the Prophet implored them, "Allah has commanded me to call you to Him. Which of you, then, will support me in this? Which of you will be my brother?"

There was silence throughout the gathering. Abu Talib did not know where to look. The two youngsters, Ja'far and Zayd, could both have spoken up, but they knew that their Islam was not in question and that the purpose of the gathering was to invite the others. But when the silence remained unbroken, thirteen-year-old Ali felt compelled to speak.

"O Prophet of Allah, I will be your supporter!"

This earned a small, barely perceptible smile from Muhammad. The Prophet laid his hand on the back of Ali's neck. "This is my brother and my supporter," he said, "so listen to him and follow him too."

There was a brief moment of murmuring before the guests rose to their feet. As they left, they looked over to Abu Talib and laughed, saying, "He's ordering us to listen to your boy and obey him."[22]

Soon, the room was empty, the dining cloths laden with pots of wasted food and drink. Abu Talib, wearing a troubled expression, turned to his nephew. Placing his hand on his shoulder like he used to when Muhammad was a boy, his uncle said, "Do what you've been ordered. By Allah, I shall always protect and defend you, but I cannot abandon the religion of Abdul Muttalib."

Although intending to raise his spirits, there was no denying that the Prophet's heart sank at these words. Nonetheless, having the protection of Abu Talib meant that he could see his mission through, and for that, he was grateful.

When the sun rose upon a new day, the streets of Makkah burst to life as the people began their day of toil and trade. With light and purposeful steps, Muhammad bypassed the braying mules heavily loaded with produce for the markets. The Prophet ascended the heights of Mount Safa. Sunlight covered every inch of the rocky hillside overlooking the Ka'bah. When he reached the very top, he raised his head and called out, "*Ya Sabahah!*"

This cry was normally used to warn citizens of impending doom, surprise attacks or other grave disasters. Commotion brewed down below as people gathered around to hear what great calamity awaited them. The Prophet spurred them on further by calling out every tribe and household by name. "O sons of Fihr! O sons of Adi! O sons of Abdu Munaf! O sons of Abdul Muttalib!" he continued calling at the top of his lungs.

The surrounding mountains carried his voice further with an echo. Those not yet present heard their names being called and rushed to the foot of Mount Safa. Those who were unable to go themselves sent someone on their behalf to see what was happening. Small talk died down as a mass of people assembled, and soon enough, many anxious eyes fixed upon *al-Amin*—the trustworthy. He was their fellow tribesman known for his sincerity, and so they knew this had to be important.

From his vantage point, the Prophet said to them: "O people of Makkah, if I were to tell you that there were some horsemen in the valley behind me planning to raid you, will you believe me?"

"Yes," they replied, bewildered at his question. "We have always found you to be honest!"

Driven by a sense of urgency, he then continued. "Well, I am here to warn you about a severe punishment that will surely fall upon you. My position is like that of someone who sees the enemy and runs to his people to warn them before they are taken by surprise, shouting as he runs: 'Beware! Beware!' This is why I cry out to you from on top of this mountain."

Abu Lahab could not contain his rage. He knew full well where this was going. Stumbling forward, he struggled to control the size of his belly under his fine garments. "*This* is what you have summoned us to hear!?" he lashed out. "May you perish from today on!"

Frustrated, he threw his hands in the air before stomping off, taking many of the other grumbling chiefs with him. Those who remained stood there in contemplation, the gravity of what the Prophet said leaving them deep in thought—*for forty years Muhammad has been such an honest person, how could we simply dismiss his words now?* However, when many of them reached home, the full realization of what Muhammad's message was calling for sat uncomfortably with them.

The elders, in particular, saw it as a direct attack on the age-old traditions and values of their forefathers, as well as a challenge to their positions of power. This was simply unheard of! What *nerve* did Muhammad have to challenge the status quo? A few chiefs from notable tribes spent a minute reflecting on his message but found it leaving them with a sour taste in their mouths. Nonetheless, those in Makkah who were not shackled by the love of power, wealth, or customs saw the beauty in the Prophet's message. The slaves of Makkah and people from the less powerful tribes found it incredibly liberating.

Although the Prophet's teachings had been behind-the-scenes for the last three years, his followers did not hesitate to speak to their trusted relatives or the people around them. Now the call was officially public— no longer a vague concept, a foolish whisper, or a rumour to be brushed off. Muhammad's teachings were now a clear and open invitation to all of the Quraysh. Day after day, the tribal chiefs became increasingly aware of the danger this new religion posed.

"This is a straightforward rebellion against our gods and customs!" barked Abu Jahl as, once again, he paced to and fro on the stone floors of Darun Nadwah. This time they were not merely annoyed—they were furious.

"He insults the beliefs of our fathers and grandfathers!" Walid frowned, curling his tawny moustache.

"He deems them misguided!" Abu Lahab's face reddened in embarrassment. "Something has to be done before this gets out of hand!" he sneered in contempt.

> *What the Prophet presented to the Arabs in the 7th century represented a revolution when compared to their own cultural norms. His message was seen as untraditional and radical— that's because it was! Today in the 21st century, the message of the Prophet continues to challenge the status quo in societies around the world on issues such as individualism, materialism, and atheism. As followers of the Prophet Muhammad, we should embrace this aspect of our religion for its very nature is to strike a clear distinction between truth and falsehood, between purity and filth—regardless of what people think.*

Chapter 8
Quraysh Take Action

It was just before sunset when a visitor knocked on the door. A soft light shone through the window, the warm glow making the face of the Prophet look even more radiant. He got up to receive his visitor. It was his uncle outside the faded wooden door.

Abu Talib, with his forehead wrinkling in worry, stepped inside quickly. He sat down before his nephew on the straw mat. A plate of caramel-coloured, juicy dates was offered to him, which he politely declined. He was much too distressed to eat. Abu Talib sighed deeply. Muhammad gazed thoughtfully at his uncle, knowing full well that he had placed him in a difficult situation. Hoping to put him at ease, he gave a warm but nervous smile.

"My dear nephew," Abu Talib began, voice heavy as he stared lovingly into the eyes of Muhammad. "Spare me and spare yourself. Please do not place upon me a burden greater than I can bear."

Even before he started speaking, the Prophet knew exactly what his uncle had come to say. It was expected. After all, the message which the Prophet and his followers were now preaching publicly caused great unrest in the city. In the last year alone, many had become outcasts in society, disowned by their families for embracing the new religion of Islam. Those who were not from powerful tribes were picked on by the likes of Abu Jahl. They were abused, and some were even tortured. With each passing day, the pressure placed on Abu Talib by the leaders of the Quraysh grew heavily.

The Prophet placed his hand softly on the thigh of his uncle. Abu Talib couldn't bear to look him in the eyes. Without the slightest hesitation, the Prophet replied firmly by saying, "I swear by God, if they put the sun in my right hand and the moon in my left on condition that I abandon this mission before Allah has made it victorious, or I have been killed, I would not abandon it."

Then, with tears in his eyes, he rose to his feet and stepped back, but his uncle seized his hand and sat him down. "My dear nephew," he said, this time more relaxed in his tone, "go ahead and do what you need to, for by God, I will never forsake you on any account."[23]

Moved by his uncle's support, the Prophet leaned forward and kissed Abu Talib on the forehead before hugging him.

§

Meanwhile, the leaders of the Quraysh came together to meet. Aggravated scowls crept over their faces as they discussed the upcoming Hajj season, their voices bouncing off the old walls of Darun Nadwah. Soon, pilgrims from all over Arabia would pour into the city, and the ever-growing number of Muslims in Makkah posed a serious problem.

Abu Jahl's thin lips curled as he snickered to himself. "Can you guess what we did to Muhammad the other day? While he was trying to pray near the Ka'bah, we gifted him with a warm surprise of camel intestines—all over his back!" He nearly crowed in delight at the memory. Eyes widened as Abu Jahl continued. "It was freshly slaughtered too, might I add. He should be grateful that we showed that etiquette at least."

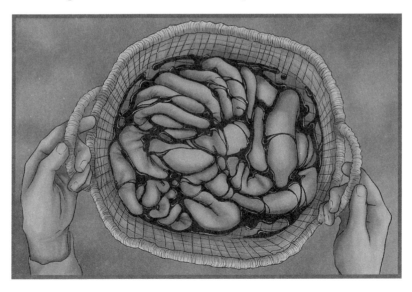

"What was his response and that of his people?" they asked, curious but also hesitant. Surely the Hashim Tribe would not have taken kindly to this gesture.

"Don't worry, none of his allies were present to see," Abu Jahl assured. His expression twisted into one of deep distaste. "He remained with his head on the ground in prostration while the waste slowly dripped off of him."

"I heard his daughter Fatimah came running to help," said Utbah.

"For someone who claims to have Allah on his side, it seems all he has is his powerless little daughter!" Abu Lahab burst out laughing and his comrades leaned slightly away to avoid the spray of spit. The red-faced chief then washed down another glass of wine, resting his next plate of food on his bulging belly as he sunk further back into his chair. Abu Lahab enjoyed this story as much as he enjoyed the delicious meals and fine wine Darun Nadwah had to offer.

"Yes, I have heard of this incident," started Walid, directing a withering gaze at his boasting accomplice. "But didn't Muhammad then stand up to you, Abu Jahl, and invoke the curse of God against you and your friends?" His eyebrows rose expectantly.

Abu Jahl's face changed colour. He cleared his throat before replying in case the worry he now felt made his voice tremble. Waving his hands dismissively in the air, he said that Muhammad's prayers would not amount to anything. However, these words did nothing to quell the rising discomfort each of them felt.

"The fact remains that his influence is growing—our children and grandchildren have been corrupted, the ways of our forefathers are being questioned and abandoned!" Utbah said, biting his nails from the side of his mouth in between sentences. "We can't even trust our slaves to be obedient anymore. The other day, Umayya almost beat his black slave to death. Wha-what's his name again?"

"Ah yes, that insolent pest, Bilal!" snapped Abu Lahab.

"Yes, him! Umayya laid him out on the scorching desert sand and placed a huge rock on his chest, yet still, that crazy man simply refused to give up the message of Muhammad. I mean, you could almost hear his back sizzling against the heat of that rock."

"I swear by Laat and Uzza, should I catch that Bilal rubbing his face in the dust in front of the Ka'bah again, I will step on his neck." A sharp thud cut through the air as Abu Jahl slammed the table for emphasis.

"Calm yourself," Abu Sufyan interjected. He was the youngest of the lot but had the wisdom of an elder.

"Even Umar faces the same problem. One of his slave girls embraced this new faith," Utbah continued, shaking his head. "It spreads amongst them like a plague, but rest assured, he beats her often to teach her a lesson!"

Some of the men hummed in approval. They commended this brutal action, pleased that one as strong and determined as Umar was as opposed to Muhammad's teachings as they were.

"Anyway, there are more pressing matters to deal with." Abu Sufyan moved their attention back to the main topic. "When the pilgrims arrive, Muhammad and his followers will certainly call them to their faith."

All the men in the meeting then turned to face Abu Sufyan as he explained how troublesome this would be. The spread of Islam would cost them not only their pride and reputation, but one of their main sources of wealth— the pilgrimage. "Have you considered how he teaches his followers that they can call out to God wherever they are?"

"You are correct! People will stop coming to Makkah if they can merely pray to their Lord from their homes!" Abu Lahab's expression soured at the realization.

"That would be preposterous!" Abu Jahl spluttered. If pilgrims from all around the Peninsula became Muslim, the Ka'bah and their idols would be rendered irrelevant. The room fell silent as the men contemplated how they would go about preventing this.

"I have an idea," said Walid after a moment. A menacing look overtook his usually grim face. "Let's announce to all the pilgrims to be wary of Muhammad. We will say that he is nothing but a liar so that they will not bother to hear him out."

Abu Sufyan disagreed. Shaking his head, he said, "Everyone knows him as *as-Sadiq al-Amin*, so then how can we claim he has suddenly gone from being honest and trustworthy to a compulsive liar?"

"Then we shall brand him a poet," said Utbah with a decisive nod.

"I am the most trained in the art of poetry. I know all of its forms," Walid stated, "and what Muhammad speaks is not mere poetry."

"Then what about calling him a fortune-teller?" Abu Lahab chimed in, keen to show the leaders of the other major tribes that he had no allegiance to his nephew. He was deeply embarrassed by his relatives— Abu Talib defended Muhammad with unwavering loyalty, and even Hamza did not reprimand his nephew, instead, carrying on as though none of this affected him. To be associated with them was almost as bad as being associated with Muhammad, Abu Lahab decided.

A weary groan interrupted the assembly from continuing. Abu Jahl had reached his limit. "Enough!" he bellowed, his voice thunderous. "This ... this is absurd! How hard can it be to silence one man!?" He clenched his teeth. "If only Abu Talib would step away and let us deal with him in a manner we see fit."

Abu Lahab's face flushed with shame while the other men raised their eyebrows at the boldness of Abu Jahl. Could he really be considering killing a leading member of the Hashim Tribe? The grandson of Abdul Muttalib, nonetheless?

Walid stood up, straightening his robe as he breathed in deeply, making his presence felt. With his back straightened and chest puffed out, he put forth his suggestion. "I've thought about this long and hard. There's only one reasonable explanation to settle this." The chamber snapped into pin-drop silence as they waited for him to continue. "The bewitching words that Muhammad sings—these verses that his followers call the Qur'an—it takes hold of their minds, affecting those who listen to it. They turn against their own families. Marriages fall apart. Family ties are destroyed. So, let us call it what it is, sorcery!"

Nodding in approval, they all agreed to this idea. If dark magic was involved, the pilgrims would surely avoid Muhammad; they would not sit in his gatherings nor listen to him. Abu Jahl grinned wickedly from ear-to-ear as he praised Walid's brilliance.

When the pilgrimage commenced, they carried out their plans with great zeal and thoroughness. Like snipers, certain men were positioned at all the main roads into Makkah, tasked with catching unsuspecting new arrivals. They would greet them and, after some small talk, would casually make mention of Muhammad and his magic. In one particular case, however, they were doomed to failure from the outset.

A Bedouin from the tribe of Ghifar named Abu Dharr visited Makkah. His tribe lived to the north-west of the city, not far from the Red Sea. He was a man searching for the truth. Unlike Amr who had embraced Islam earlier, Abu Dharr had already heard of the Prophet and his message of worshipping the one true God without partners. Like most of his tribesmen, he was a highwayman, pillaging caravans and seeking out vulnerable travellers to rob. However, unlike his people, he was a firm believer in the Oneness of God and refused to pay any respect to idols. What sparked Abu Dharr's quest to leave his village in search of

Muhammad was when his brother Unays returned from Makkah with news of a man who claimed to be a Prophet.

"And what does this Prophet from the Quraysh call to?" Abu Dharr asked, at first sceptical.

Unays explained, "This man says that there is no God worthy of worship except Allah." He noticed his brother's eyes suddenly brighten. "But just know that his people are quickly turning against him."

Despite his brother's warning, Abu Dharr immediately set off for Makkah with full certainty that this was a true Prophet. Upon his arrival, the men stationed at the entrances to Makkah—as per the instructions of Walid and the other leaders—warned him not to go near the powerful magician named Muhammad. The Bedouin nodded away but had no intention of listening to them. In fact, the warning made him all the more intrigued to meet this man.

Hurriedly, he made his way further into the city to ask about the new Prophet. The people's reaction was abrupt and rude—he soon realized that talk of Muhammad was not going to be tolerated. After some days of lying low and investigating, Abu Dharr established contact with one of the Prophet's closest Companions. Ali had befriended him, and when the time was right, he took Abu Dharr to meet the Prophet Muhammad.

They found him sleeping soundly on a bench in the courtyard, his handsome face covered by a fold of his cloak. A few men lingered nearby, quietly conversing amongst themselves. Without hesitation, Abu Dharr woke the Prophet and wished him good morning.

"Peace be upon you!" replied the Prophet as he sat up. He smiled at his guest. "Where are you from?"

Abu Dharr told him that he was from the infamous tribe of Ghifar, well known for being thugs. He watched the Prophet bring his hand to his forehead in a gesture of surprise.

I knew it. He dislikes that I am from Ghifar! Abu Dharr concluded to himself.

He stretched out his hand to hold onto the Prophet's, hoping to assure him that this was no thoughtless visit, but a Companion was quick to slap it away. By now the Prophet's followers had become very protective over him. They were wary of the dangers he now faced, more so, having learned that their new visitor belonged to a ruthless tribe. Despite this, the Prophet continued to warmly converse with Abu Dharr, expressing interest in the man's story.

"How long have you been in Makkah for?"

"Almost 30 days."

"And who has been feeding you all this time?"

"All I've been having here is the water from the well of Zam Zam," Abu Dharr confessed. "I cannot believe it! I have *put on* weight and started to see my stomach become flabby!" Abu Dharr pinched his side, squeezing his fattening waist.

"It is truly just as good as food! It is blessed," the Prophet confirmed.

"Tell me about this Islam," said the Bedouin, cutting straight to the point.

Although his mannerisms were direct, the Prophet could sense his curiosity was genuine. "I am no poet," said the Prophet, "but what I recite is the Qur'an, and it is not I who speaks but Allah."

"Recite for me," said Abu Dharr.

The Prophet nodded gracefully and then recited a portion. The beauty of the words overcame Abu Dharr so much that right then and there, he declared, "I testify that there is no God worthy of worship except Allah, and that Muhammad is the Messenger of God!"[24]

"Now return to your people, Abu Dharr, and keep this matter to yourself," the Prophet instructed him. "Later on, when you hear of my victory, return to me." This was the strategy that he took with followers from afar.

"I swear by God," Abu Dharr said, raising his voice and shaking his head out of excitement, "I must announce this to all!"

The other Companions tried to stop him, but Abu Dharr was strong-minded. He marched over to the Ka'bah, his sandals leaving deep imprints in the sandy streets. In full view of everyone, he made his announcement.

"O people of Quraysh! I bear witness that there is no God worthy of worship except Allah!" Heads turned. People edged closer to listen, the crowd curious to see what this stranger from out of town was so eager to say. "...And I bear witness that Muhammad is the slave and Messenger of God!" he continued at the top of his voice.

Curiosity quickly turned into anger. The people closed in on Abu Dharr, who soon found himself at the centre of some rather hostile attention.

"He's a *Sabi*, get him!" yelled a shrill voice in the crowd. The Quraysh had recently come up with this insulting label for the Muslims—*Sabi* meant heretic. Barely a moment later, the people rushed to beat Abu Dharr in a mob-like frenzy. They were merciless. They punched, kicked, and stomped on him till his knees buckled. He would have died that day had it not been for the Prophet's uncle, Abbas, who rushed to his defence.

"Do you not know his tribe is the infamous Ghifar?" Abbas exclaimed, leaning over Abu Dharr's body to shield him. "What do you think they will do to you when they find out a man of theirs was killed by you!?"[25]

At this, the crowd dispersed, all while muttering insults under their breath. Abu Dharr stood up, bloodied and in a daze. He dusted himself off and looked at the shrines surrounding him. The soulless idols seemed to stare back blankly, mockingly. Instead of heading home, he decided to stay for one final night in Makkah. The following day, to the surprise of everyone, he made the same announcement and the incident unfolded in the same way with Abbas coming to the rescue once again.

Soon after, Abu Dharr returned home. His negative experience with the Quraysh did not reduce his resolve, for his faith was firm and true. Abu Dharr shared the message of Islam with his people with as much pride as he did in Makkah, his story capturing their imagination, and the message of the Prophet inevitably entering their hearts.

Meanwhile, in Makkah, the rumour that Muhammad was a sorcerer spread throughout the city and beyond as the visiting pilgrims returned to their homes. The smear campaign gained traction and the Prophet soon witnessed people openly mock and hurl abuse at him. People challenged him to present miracles and proofs, and he tirelessly answered by quoting the Qur'an and saying, "I am simply a messenger!"

Throughout Makkah, group loyalties stretched to breaking point as dissent over Muhammad's message began to split families apart. After the respected Abu Bakr had accepted Islam, his wife and two of his adult children followed his example, but one son remained stubbornly opposed. And despite Khadijah's half-brother being one of Muhammad's most bitter opponents, his own two sons were divided. One was a passionate believer, while the other held back despite being married to Muhammad and Khadijah's eldest daughter. Before long, under the pressure of his tribe, he divorced her.

As animosity grew, verbal abuse eventually turned physical. Yet, the intensity of abuse only increased the Prophet's forbearance. Driven by his desire to protect his community, Prophet Muhammad was determined to make God's message prevail. He started to consider all of his options.

Chapter 9
Strategic Thinking

Despite the ongoing persecution in Makkah, the Prophet continued to visit the Ka'bah to say his prayers. His followers could only watch from a distance and admire his courage.

One day, while some of the leaders of Quraysh sat in the shade of the sacred cube-shaped building, bitterly stirring up each other's anger against Muhammad, it so happened that the Prophet himself entered the sanctuary. He was instantly recognizable amidst the other people passing by. Moderate height, wavy dark hair, and straightened shoulders, Muhammad made for a striking image in his white robe and neatly-wrapped turban. Going to the east corner of the Ka'bah, he kissed the Black Stone and began to make the seven rounds in worship.

As he passed the semi-circle short wall adjacent to the Ka'bah, they raised their voices and shamelessly poked fun at him. It was clear from his face that he had heard what they said. He passed them again on his second round, and again they slandered him. Although their taunts were hurtful, his response was to remain silent. Without uttering a word, he looked at them before continuing his walk at a measured pace, neither hastening nor slowing down. He wanted his followers to know that evil should not be responded to with evil.

On his third circuit, they began insulting his religion and mocking Allah. At this, he unexpectedly stopped in his tracks. Raising his head while turning to the jeering crowd, the Prophet exclaimed, "O People of Quraysh! Listen to me, I swear by Allah in Whose Hand is my soul, you will one day be torn to shreds."

The men were stunned. The certainty of his words overcame them, snatching away their ability to speak, for his prayers scared them and sent a chill down their spines. The uncomfortable silence was finally broken by Abu Jahl.

"Go on with your business, Muhammad," he said, trying not to provoke him further, "by God, you are not an ignorant person."

The Prophet continued making his rounds. They watched him leave before grumbling amongst themselves.

"He may have caught us by surprise this time, but mark my words, it *won't* happen again."

"Indeed, we fear no one. And we won't be so tolerant next time," said Abu Jahl through gritted teeth.

They vowed that soon they would make amends for this momentary display of weakness. Despite the brightness of the midday sun, a dark cloud of resentment overshadowed each of them as they parted ways to their spacious homes.

§

Abu Jahl felt sure of succeeding his uncle to become the chief of the Makhzum Tribe, the second most powerful tribe in Makkah. After all, he had already established for himself a certain position in society through his wealth and flamboyant parties and feasts, and partly also through making himself feared through his ruthlessness and readiness to take revenge on anyone who opposed him.

He had been the most unrelenting of all those men who had been stationed at the approaches to Makkah during the recent pilgrimage. He was the most vocal in his criticism of the Prophet as a dangerous sorcerer. He was also the most active in persecuting the more helpless believers of his own tribe and urging other tribes to do the same. But one day, in a surprising twist of fate, he indirectly did the budding religion a great service.

The Prophet was sitting deep in thought some distance away from the Ka'bah at the foot of Mount Safa, the place where he had bravely taken his message public for the first time. It seemed like just yesterday, although almost three years of hardship and pain had since gone by. He was alone at this holy place when Abu Jahl came past. Abu Jahl's eyes brightened in cunning delight—here was an opportunity for him to prove that Muhammad's prayer a few days earlier had not scared him in the least!

Standing in front of the Prophet, the imposing tribe leader proceeded to revile him with all the abusive words he could muster. The Prophet, a man of great patience, merely looked at him but spoke not a word. After having heaped upon him the worst insults he could think of, Abu Jahl casually strolled off towards the Ka'bah to sit with his friends as though he had accomplished a great task. The Prophet quietly rose to his feet and returned to his home.

He had scarcely gone—his sandal-prints still fresh in the sand—when Hamza, his uncle and senior by four years, appeared in the opposite direction. Hamza was on his way back from a hunting trip, sitting atop his chestnut-coloured horse, which smoothly strutted into the area. Known as the strongest man in Quraysh, he was seldom seen without his famous bow slung over his shoulder. This great warrior was headed towards the sacred building in the middle of the city—it was his habit to visit the Ka'bah to pay his respects before returning home. Upon seeing him, a servant woman rushed out of a home near Mount Safa.

"O Hamza!" she called, so enraged by what she had witnessed that she could barely speak. "If only you had seen ... seen how Muhammad—your sweet nephew—was treated by Abu Jahl just moments earlier!"

The woman's frantic plea stopped Hamza in his tracks, and he slid down the side of his horse without a moment to waste. "What did you say about Muhammad?" he asked before his feet hit the ground.

Visibly upset, she conveyed every part that she had heard, receiving Hamza's undivided attention as she spoke. "He found him sitting here," she said, pointing at a rock where the Prophet had been moments earlier, "and insulted him using the cruellest words imaginable. And Muhammad, well, he didn't even say a word back. Then Abu Jahl just left—" She half-gestured by tilting her head in the direction of the Ka'bah where Abu Jahl now sat with his comrades.

Hamza had a generally approachable and easy-going temperament. Nonetheless, he was the most headstrong of the Quraysh, and when provoked, was certainly the most formidable and stern. His mighty frame now shook with anger at how his nephew had been abused in such an unprovoked manner. Striding into the sanctuary of the Ka'bah, he made straight for Abu Jahl. People standing in conversation or prayer stumbled out of the way when Hamza marched through, his stride and demeanour resembling that of a lion on the prowl. Standing over Abu Jahl, he raised his bow high and brought it down in full force onto the unsuspecting man. Abu Jahl yelped, his back stinging from the powerful blow. He looked around wildly to see who it was.

"Will you insult him..." Hamza said, towering over the startled body of Abu Jahl, and then as much to his own amazement as anyone else's, he heard himself saying, "...now that I am of his religion, and now that I vouch for what he vouches? Strike me blow for blow if you dare!"

His bold words engulfed everyone within earshot. A spasm of fear flicked across Abu Jahl's face. A hush descended as onlookers, rooted in their place, watched on expectantly. Abu Jahl was not one lacking in courage and, surrounded by his comrades, could easily have fought back, but he thought better of it. Even by his lowly standards, what he had done to Muhammad had crossed a line, for he was, after all, from the prestigious Hashim Tribe. To dishonour one from them was an insult to all of them. So when his fellow tribesmen rose to their feet to help, he motioned them to stand down.

"Let Hamza be, for by God, I reviled his nephew in the ugliest way possible," he confessed.

The men backed down, not before scoffing at Hamza, "So, we see you're turning into a heretic too!"

"And *who's* going to stop me?" demanded Hamza.

His fiery gaze intimidated the men, who quickly dispersed, cursing him under their breath and taking their wounded tribesman with them. The prideful Abu Jahl hit away their supportive hands and instead chose to walk alone, forcing his posture as upright as he could without flinching. The pain pulsating down his back was slowly dwarfed by the realization that this incident would be a great victory to Muhammad and his message—Hamza's conversion would only strengthen his position and increase his protection! He had thought he was hurting Muhammad but instead, his harassment caused a powerful man of Quraysh to embrace the religion. This bitter realization overpowered any remaining shred of self-satisfaction he had.

Meanwhile, another realization struck as soon as Hamza returned home. As his anger slowly subsided, he realized what he had done in the heat of the moment. *You, a leader amongst the Quraysh, have followed this rebel and abandoned the religion of your forefathers! Death is best for you for what you've done!* [26] Doubts of this nature set in as he sat there in thought, not knowing what to do.

The next morning, he went to see Muhammad, seeking advice for his dilemma. "Dearest nephew, I've fallen into a trap from which I do not know how to escape. I do not know whether continuing as I am is wiser for me or whether it will be a terrible mistake. Please talk to me. What should I do?"

The Prophet listened to Hamza's retelling of the incident and then took his time speaking to his uncle, counselling him, and reassuring him about his decision to leave idol worship in favour of Islam. By the time he had finished saying what he wanted to, Hamza's stony expression had thawed, now replaced by a thoughtful gaze.

Voice firm, his uncle responded, "I do truly bear witness that you are telling the truth. Continue with your mission, my nephew, for by God, I would not like to own a single thing under the sky while keeping to my former religion."

Prophet Muhammad smiled ear-to-ear at his uncle's resolve.

Hamza becoming a Muslim soon became the talk of the town, though none dared to confront him head-on. Frustrated by their inability to stop Islam from spreading, the leaders of the Quraysh became ruthless in their persecution of the Prophet's followers. They eagerly resorted to any means of torture that they could think of: beating their victims, starving them, lying them out on the baking hot sand ... the methods were as plentiful as they were cruel. Their primary aim was to force the Muslims to abandon their religion.

Determined to protect the faith of his followers, the Prophet began considering his options. He considered sending a number of them away to live elsewhere until the situation had improved. Weighing up the pros and cons of all the potential areas, he came to a decision. The ideal place needed to be far away enough to stop the Quraysh from meddling in their affairs, yet familiar enough to be sure that his followers would be welcomed. Although their safety was his top priority, he also considered the advantage of having a separate group of believers practicing and teaching Islam in another land. If the community flourished, gaining allies and spreading the truth, they would surely become an invaluable support to the main body of Muslims in Makkah. With this in mind, he called for a secret meeting at Darul Arqam, the house of the Companion Arqam.

His followers gathered quietly in the night. They tried hiding their scars and bruises from the eyes of their Prophet, not wanting to burden him any more than he already was. Some would only look downwards, avoiding his gaze in case he noticed the pain in their eyes. When they glanced at the Prophet's expression, they saw that his usually soft features carried the weight of a life-changing announcement. Still, he welcomed them with comforting warmth as they gathered before him.

They listened intently as he told them to head to Abyssinia in North Africa, the home of a Christian community and a place often visited by the Arabs for business.

"If you go to the land of the Abyssinians, you will find there a king in whose kingdom no one is wronged," the Prophet said. He had thought long and hard before advising them to migrate. The situation in Makkah was worsening by the day, and there was little he could do to protect everyone. "You should remain there until the Almighty opens up a way of relief and removes the suffering."

The Companions, sensing the heaviness in his voice, knew that such a decision had not been taken without serious consideration, for one of those encouraged to migrate was the Prophet's own daughter, Ruqayya. Her presence, along with her husband Uthman, would become a source of great strength for the entire group that would migrate. Although it would pain them to leave their home, the Companions left the meeting understanding full well that nothing in this world was more precious than faith and that sacrifices would be needed in order to protect it.

Ruqayya was amongst the last to leave the meeting place. The Prophet bid his daughter farewell with a kiss on the forehead. Closing her eyes, she breathed in his unforgettable pleasant scent that came from his wavy hair, treasuring the embrace and his words of comfort. She did not know if she would ever see him again.

Soon, it was time for the first batch of sixteen Companions to embark on the first *hijrah*, or migration, in Islam. These brave men and women slipped out of town with nothing but their faith and a few horses and camels for their journey to the closest port town. They left behind everything they knew and held dear, and upon arriving at the salt-scented port, their eyes filled with tears when realizing just how far away they would be from the Prophet and the Revelation from Allah.

Ja'far, the brother of Ali and a cousin of the Prophet, imparted words of hope to reassure the Companions as they boarded one of the boats. With heavy yet hopeful hearts, they crossed over the vast Red Sea into the land of Abyssinia, setting the course for another migration that would take place sometime later when another eighty-three men and nineteen women would follow. The Quraysh could have stopped their migration if they had known about it, but the Prophet's strategic move had been unexpected, and they failed to realize what had happened until the believers had already reached their destination.

When the boat eventually drew near the port of Abyssinia, the sight of tall columns reaching for the cloudless blue sky greeted them. The Prophet had been right in his prediction. Not only did they find safety in this Abyssinian Kingdom, but their new neighbours soon warmed to them, and the king, known as a Najashi, was touched by the story of Muhammad.

One day, shortly after arriving, Ruqayya and a few female Companions stood in line at a stall that was bustling as townspeople bargained to get their produce. The stall owner was an elderly lady, her bright garments contrasting with her blank expression as she watched the Muslims step up to her table. She was worried they would attempt to con her, as had been her experience with many foreigners.

Ruqayya was the first to greet, smiling politely. "I hope that the day finds you in good health, God-willing."

The Abyssinian woman blinked in surprise—not many of her customers wished her well, much less remember to greet her. "You are new here," she said carefully.

Ruqayya nodded.

"Where are you all from?" she addressed the group of unfamiliar faces.

"We come from Makkah," one of the women answered. "We heard that the lands of Abyssinia are blessed with the sweetest of fruits. May we purchase from you?"

The elderly lady nodded, smiling a little. "You heard correctly."

Impressed by their kind faces and good manners, she gestured at what remained of the fruits and vegetables decorating the table. The very best had already been sold. "If you can wait for a while, I will send for a fresh basket from my farm."

Pleased by the kind offer, they agreed to wait, standing aside as the woman assigned the task to her grandchildren playing nearby. A while later, they left the marketplace with containers full of fruit and hearts full of optimism—life in Abyssinia was looking bright.

Meanwhile, the Quraysh gathered together with darkened expressions. They were furious upon discovering that some Muslims had secretly left the city, for among those who migrated were the sons and daughters of many of the leading families of Makkah. Their anger was even greater when they found out that these Muslims had been warmly welcomed in Abyssinia—one of their key trading partners. Quickly, they mustered up a plan to have them all rounded up and dragged back to Makkah. They appointed two highly skilled politicians to set sail with a caravan brimming with bribes.

"Amr al-Aas is an expert wordsmith. His words will impress the Najashi perhaps more than these exquisite gifts." They smiled. The plan left no stone unturned ... or so they thought.

When the ship arrived on the coast, the townspeople gathered, eyes wide in awe at the load of precious items transported off the ship. A woman carrying a vessel filled with water nearly dropped it as her eyes were drawn to the polished lamps, glittering trinkets, beautifully designed earthenware, and baskets filled with a variety of dates. A few bribes later, the delegates from Quraysh quickly gained an audience with the Najashi, who smiled widely upon welcoming them. He was especially pleased by the leather products gifted to him—a clever choice by the Quraysh as they knew how sought-after leatherwork was in Abyssinia.

With a lavish bow, Amr Al-Aas, dressed in striking blue and red garments, began his plea: "O King! Some fools from our homeland have taken refuge in your country."

"Do you refer to the small group that arrived here not too long ago?" the Najashi asked.

"Indeed! Although I am embarrassed to be associated with them." Amr admitted, sighing deeply. "They have abandoned our religion, and instead of accepting yours, they have invented their own. And so our leaders have sent us to bring them back home so that we may deal with them appropriately."

The clergy vouched for Amr's plight, but the Najashi was a fair man. "I would prefer it if I heard both sides of the story," he said, and then sent for the Muslims to make their case.

The sudden summons worried them, but they decided to approach the situation with only the truth and wisdom, electing Ja'far to take charge. Leading the group, Ja'far humbly entered Najashi's court. The chamber was as long as it was spacious, a gentle breeze blowing in from the narrow windows. Lamps of bronze hung from the ceiling, and burning torches were fixed against intricately carved stone pillars that lead all the way to the throne. The guards stood on either end of the room, boasting round shields and spears that were as tall as they. The clergy hovered nearby, robed men of varying sizes wearing golden crosses over their necks.

They frowned when Ja'far politely nodded in greeting instead of prostrating in the presence of royalty. Najashi rose from his throne. He nudged his jewel-encrusted staff in the immigrants' direction. "Tell me, why have you forsaken the religion of your people and abandoned your tribes?"

Ja'far stepped forward. "O King! We were a people steeped in ignorance and savagery. We worshipped idols while neglecting family and the rights of our neighbours. We committed many atrocities, and the strong would regularly oppress the weak," he explained.

The two delegators from Makkah moved to interrupt, but Najashi raised his hand and then reclined in his seat, listening with interest.

Ja'far passionately continued, "We were in this pitiful state until God chose from amongst us a man whose lineage, truthfulness, and purity we knew very well. Prophet Muhammad called to worship One God alone. He advised us to speak the truth, to be merciful, to uphold the rights of family and neighbours. He forbade us to mistreat women or to eat the property of orphans, and he commanded us to offer prayers, to give in charity, and to fast. So we believed in his message and followed him, worshipping Allah alone."

He briefly glanced at the Quraysh delegates, who were staring at him, completely unimpressed by his speech. "But our people treated us with violence and persecution to force us to return to idol worship. The situation became unbearable, and so we have come to your country with the hope that you, a just ruler, will protect us from oppression."

The Najashi leaned forward with eyes full of intrigue as he asked, "Do you have any Revelation with you that this Prophet says he brought?"

Ja'far nodded, composed himself, and then began to recite. His wisdom directed him to recite from the Chapter of Mary, an intelligent choice given the Christian audience. His rich, melodious voice told the story of the miraculous birth of Jesus. His recitation stirred hearts. Tears rolled down Najashi's cheeks, soaking his beard. Even the clergy with pockets full of bribes found their eyes welling up with emotion.

"It seems as if these words and those which were revealed to Jesus are rays of light coming from the same lamp," Najashi mused aloud before turning to the frowning delegates. "You may go. I am afraid I cannot return these people. They are under my protection."

Ruqayya smiled to herself as she recalled the words of her father in the house of Arqam: "A king in whose kingdom no one is wronged."

As always, her father's words were truthful.

Disappointed, Amr al-Aas and his Companion left the court. They needed to switch tactics. "We will try again tomorrow."

"Neither the gifts nor the bribes to the clergy amounted to anything … so what are we to do now?"

Amr thought for a moment. "We will tell Najashi what Muhammad and his people think of Jesus. That they deny Jesus and reduce him to nothing but a slave. That should rattle his cage."

The very next day, they conveyed this and more, which concerned Najashi deeply. Being a religious man, he could not tolerate blasphemy in his kingdom. Once again, the Muslim immigrants were summoned. The group entered, again without bowing.

"See, they do not even respect you enough to prostrate!" Amr mentioned.

"Our Prophet taught us not to prostrate to man. We bow only to the Creator," explained Ja'far.

Najashi nodded, letting the matter slide—he was more concerned with what they believed about Jesus. He asked them to explain, watching them very carefully. Amr smirked at his comrade, who winked back enthusiastically, both thinking they had cornered the Muslims.

"We say about Jesus what our Prophet has taught us." Ja'far understood the sensitive nature of this question and chose his next words carefully. "He taught us that Jesus is the servant of God, the Messenger of God, the Word of God cast upon Mary, the chaste."

Amr's face grew into a frown. He was silently hoping the Muslims would zealously proclaim they didn't believe Jesus to be the son of God, but Ja'far had intelligently mentioned everything about him *except* that point.

Najashi stood quietly for a moment. Everyone waited with bated breath. Leaning on his staff, he bent to pick up a short piece of straw from the ground. "The difference between what you say about him and what I say about him does not exceed the length of this straw," he said while holding it up before his eyes.

Realizing their precious gifts were now at risk, the clergy protested, closely followed by some of the generals, but their king's mind was already set. The delegates from Makkah found their frowns deepening all the more when the king assured the Muslims that they were welcome to practice their new religion.

"They are free to live and worship in my land as they please," the Najashi said with finality, ordering his attendants to return all of the gifts sent by Quraysh. He then bid the delegates farewell, leaving no room for protest.

The relief felt by the Muslims in Abyssinia that day was in stark contrast to the dreadful situation that the Muslims in Makkah would soon come to face.

Chapter 10
All Alone

When the two delegates returned to Makkah, the look on their faces said it all. The disappointing news spread quickly, sparking outrage amongst the leaders of Quraysh. Immediately, they set about intensifying their persecution of the believers, largely under the direction of Abu Jahl, whose nephew Umar was one of the most violent and strict in carrying out his instructions. If there was one man Abu Jahl could rely on not to tolerate any monotheistic nonsense, it was his nephew.

Still in his twenties, Umar was known for his quickness with a whip and his sharp temper. His imposing physique made people all the more fearful of him. But unlike his uncle, he was sincere, and this was precisely the reason why he opposed the new religion so staunchly. After all, his father Khattab had brought him up to venerate the Ka'bah and to respect everything that had come to be inseparably connected with it in the way of idols and ancient traditions.

Makkah was now a city of two religions, the community divided. Any semblance of unity between the people was now no more, and this concerned Umar. He saw clearly that the trouble had one cause only— remove the man who was that cause, and everything would soon be as it had been before. Thoughts of this nature festered in his mind for some time and, not long after the unsuccessful return of the delegates, they erupted. Umar snapped into action. In a turbulent wave of anger, he grabbed his sword, marching out of his house. The blade gleamed menacingly in the daylight as he headed straight for the Prophet's house. He had had enough.

Along the way, Umar came face to face with Nu'aym, a fellow tribesman. Nu'aym had entered Islam but kept it a secret in fear of how people like Umar would react. The incensed expression on Umar's face prompted him to ask where he was going. Umar barely spared him a passing glance.

"I am going to Muhammad, that traitor who has split the Quraysh into two and insulted our gods," he said furiously, without pausing in his steps, "and I shall kill him."

Nu'aym's eyes widened. He hastened forward. "Don't do it, Umar! His followers will kill you before any harm comes to their man."

He warned Umar of the consequences, yet Umar was unaffected by such an argument. Quickly, he thought of another way by which he might at least delay Umar in time to warn the Prophet. This idea would mean betraying fellow Muslims who, like himself, were concealing their Islam; but he knew that they would forgive him and even commend him, given the circumstances.

"O Umar!" he called, rushing to catch up with him. "Why not first deal with the people of your own household?" he blurted out.

Umar's eyes narrowed in disdain. He spun around with a deep frown, saying, "What *people* of my household?"

"Your brother-in-law Sa'id and your sister Fatimah."

Without a word, Umar's grip tightened around the handle of his sword, his brisk walk now aimed toward his sister's place. The clay house stood innocently in the neighbourhood, its windows draped shut, keeping its inhabitants peacefully unaware of the storm coming their way. As Umar approached, he heard murmurs coming from inside. Someone was reciting what sounded like a prayer. His heavy footsteps scattered stray pebbles out of the way, alerting them of his approach, and by the time he reached the door, the gentle melodious sound had been replaced with clamour and commotion.

As Umar stormed in, Fatimah and Sa'id stood up as though struck by lightning. Fatimah quickly tucked the parchment from which they had been reciting behind her back.

"What is that nonsensical chanting I heard coming from inside here?"

"It is nothing, my brother. We were just ... talking."

"I clearly heard something," he said sternly, his eyes now fixed on Sa'id's worried face.

They eyed his threatening sword and nervously asked, "What brings you here, Umar?"

"I am told that you both have become followers of Muhammad."

Their panicked expressions said it all. Before either of them could speak a word, Umar stretched his hands out towards his brother-in-law's neck and leapt at him. Sa'id's back met the wall with a dull thud. Nearby pots fell over, cracking as they hit the ground, caught in between the assault. Fatimah rushed to intervene.

"Get off, Umar!" she shrieked.

In a fit of rage, Umar struck out, hitting her across the face. The force sent her tumbling to the ground. "It's true!" Fatimah cried aloud, wiping the blood now trickling down the side of her face. Looking straight up at her brother, she held back the tears as she defiantly said, "We've embraced the new religion and believe in Allah and His Messenger... So do whatever you want!"

Umar realized what he had done, and shame overcame him. The room was disturbed, and so were his relatives. His sister slowly pulled herself up from the floor, her hand gingerly touching her injury. His heart softened and his tone lowered, "Show me the parchment you were reading from." He stretched out his hand, waiting expectantly. "I want to see for myself what this Muhammad has been saying."

Umar, like the other two, was one of the few people in Makkah who could read. To his surprise, he was met with an abrupt reply. "No. We are scared you may destroy it," said Fatimah.

"Fear not," he said, sensing their caution. Unbuckling his belt, he lay down his sword, swearing by his gods that he would give it back after reading it.

Fatimah could see that he had settled down, and at the same time, she longed for her brother to see the beauty of Islam. "My brother, your idol worship has made you impure. Before touching this, you must wash," she explained.

Umar, now curious and sufficiently calm, went and washed himself. He then took hold of the parchment, a thin beige sheet made from animal skin. Lifting it close to his face, his eyes scanned across the Arabic verses, pausing at the end of each line to reflect. Inscribed on the parchment was the opening of Surah Ta-Ha:

Ta Ha—We have not revealed the Quran to you O Prophet to cause you distress, but as a reminder to those in awe of Allah.

A revelation from the One who created the earth and the high heaven—the Most Compassionate, Who is established on the Throne.

To Him belongs whatever is in the heavens and whatever is on the earth and whatever is in between and whatever is underground. Whether you speak openly or not, He certainly knows what is secret and what is even more hidden.

Allah—there is no god worthy of worship except Him. He has the Most Beautiful Names.

[Qur'an 20: 1–8]

When Umar reached the end, he looked up in wonderment. "How beautiful and noble are these words!"

Fatimah and Sa'id, now standing side by side, smiled softly. "Do you now see what we see?"

"Where is Muhammad right now?" Umar asked. "I must see him at once!"

His eyes now shone with interest instead of fury. They recognized that expression and deemed it safe to send him on his way to the meeting place of the Muslims. Umar buckled up his waist strap once more, and with his hand gripping the handle of his sword, marched over to Darul Arqam. He knocked urgently on the door. Those inside had been warned by Nu'aym, but nothing could have prepared them for what was about to unfold.

"It is me, the son of Khattab," Umar's voice announced before the knocking resumed. "Open the door."

The men inside were struck by the subdued tone of his usually commanding voice. They presumed it was all part of his plan to fool them into letting him in. One of the men peered through a chink in the wooden door and what he saw made him step back in dismay.

"O Messenger of Allah," he reported, "it is Umar with ... with his hand placed firmly on his sword."

At this, anxiety rippled through the air. Many in that chamber shared the man's fears—but not Hamza. "Let him come in," he said firmly, now standing directly between the door and in front of the Prophet. "If he has come with good intentions, we will show him goodness. If his intent is evil, we will slay him with his own sword."

The Prophet then gave permission to let Umar in. The men at the door did so cautiously. The door slowly creaked open and soon Umar's head peered into the chamber. He had barely set foot in the chamber when the Prophet stood up and paced towards him. He grabbed Umar by his belt and pulled him into the middle of the room forcefully. The Companions stared in awe. Umar, known for his bold and fierce nature, was almost twice his size, yet the Prophet appeared unfazed by this.

"What has brought you here, O son of Khattab?" he asked, his voice urgent. "Will it take a Divine punishment for you to stop with this opposition?"

"O Messenger of Allah, I have come to you to declare my faith in Allah, in His Messenger, and in what he has brought from Allah," said Umar.

The Companions listened in disbelief. Had Umar, one of the strongest opponents of Islam, really just declared his faith!?

"*Allahu Akbar*!" the Prophet said aloud, and every person in the building then knew without a doubt that Umar had embraced Islam.[27] They all rejoiced, echoing the Prophet's words such that the streets resonated with their cheer.

There was no question of Umar keeping his faith a secret. He wanted everyone to know, particularly those who were the most hostile towards Muhammad. And so, the very next morning, he knocked on the door of the Prophet's fiercest enemy—Abu Jahl. The tribe leader came out, straightening his lavish robe before greeting Umar.

"The best of welcomes to my nephew! What brings you here?"

"I came to tell you that I believe in Allah and in His Messenger, Muhammad," Umar stated calmly. "And I testify to the truth of that which he has brought."

Taken aback, Abu Jahl's mouth flapped open and shut wordlessly. He then thrust an accusing finger, waving it at the bold young man in front of him. "May the gods curse you!" he shrieked. "And may their curse be on this horrid news you have brought!"

And with that, he slammed the door in Umar's face.[28]

§

"So much for your master plan, Walid!" snapped Abu Jahl, dropping into his seat with a grunt. To describe him as annoyed would be an understatement.

The leaders of the Quraysh were seething. It was one thing after another. Their plans to undermine the Prophet by making him out to be a sorcerer had clearly not done the trick, and now Hamza and Umar's conversion in quick succession only added fuel to the already raging fire.

"First Hamza, and now Umar... Who's next?"

After those two powerful Quraysh members joined their movement, the Muslims seemed emboldened and would even dare to come out in public to worship. The audacity sickened these scheming leaders who were still reeling from the embarrassment of Abyssinia.

"Time for my plan of action," Abu Jahl addressed the brooding men in the room. "Listen carefully and listen well. We will cut them off, every last one of them."

"Do you mean to propose a boycott?"

Abu Jahl nodded, his face taut and grim. Their eyes lit up at this ingenious idea.

"Nobody should have any dealings of any kind with members of the Hashim Tribe, not even for basic foodstuffs. Let them all starve for their so-called Prophet!" he thundered on, almost frothing at the mouth with anger when thinking about how some of the Muslims had found a safe haven in Abyssinia.

"May I add to that," Abu Sufyan interjected, not wanting to be outdone by Abu Jahl's cunningness, "they should be barred from the caravans, banned from the markets, and excluded from all business partnerships."

Abu Jahl's poisonous rhetoric seemed to have swayed the usually more sensible Abu Sufyan, at least for now. Walid crossed his arms, cupping his chin in one hand, deep in thought. "Yes. And for good measure, I say no member of any tribe can marry one of them. Let us make them feel as though they do not exist!"

Abu Lahab let out a throaty sigh. "The problem lies not only with my nephew and his band of followers." He flicked away the tawny bone of his third drumstick, shaking his head hopelessly. "Abu Talib is a tremendous pain. He may not follow their ways, but he offers them the protection of both the Hashim and Muttalib Tribes."

"He is only helping to spread his nephew's evil!" Utbah agreed.

"Then we boycott them as well!" remarked Walid casually with a decisive nod. He raised his right hand high, pointing a finger to the ceiling, the ruby in his ring capturing the candlelight nearby. "Unless they hand Muhammad over to be killed or replace Abu Talib with someone who will, then they *all* will have to bear the brunt of it."

Abu Jahl's enthusiasm mounted as their plan began to take shape. He now sat more upright in his seat. "We will accept no bargains for peace whether by man, woman, or child until they all abandon Muhammad."

Their words were especially vicious and the cruelty of their scheme barely registered, after all, desperate times called for desperate measures...

"So, are we all in agreement to see this through?" Abu Sufyan asked.

A few eyes glanced at Abu Lahab, who held up his hands and promptly distanced himself from his nephew and his tribe. "I am with you all. In fact, let us not waste any time and implement this at the first light of dawn!"

Immediately, they had the declaration committed to writing, inscribed on parchment made of sheepskin, and sealed by the leaders of the two largest tribes—Abu Jahl of the Makhzum and Abu Sufyan of the Umayyads. They agreed to drag every tribe member of Hashim and Muttalib from their homes and bar them from returning; the boycott would extend to every one of them, the followers and the sympathizers, all who associated with Muhammad.

The news broke as soon as dawn did. The notice was nailed to the door of the Ka'bah, and Abu Jahl's men announced the boycott loud and clear as they set out to forcibly collect every person belonging to the two tribes, waving copies of the policy in the startled faces of women and children.

Even the elders were not spared from the brutality and mockery. Abu Talib did all he could, stretching his resources thin to provide shelter for everyone. Expelled from the comfort of their homes, the people were forced to pitch tents in the nearby Valley of Shi'b, a place so narrow it was barely wide enough for a camel to wander freely.

The Prophet, Khadijah, and their children carried what little belongings they could manage in their arms. Anyone who stood around to taunt them along the way was startled by the dignity surrounding the family as they walked on in quiet patience to the tent that would be their home for the next two years.

Everyday life became a struggle, one that extended beyond the effort to secure food and meet other basic needs. Being shunned ate at the people's self-respect. The pleasantries of casual encounters in the street, the leisurely give-and-take of buying and selling in the market, the camaraderie of discussion and consultation in the shade of the Ka'bah— all the small things that made up the feeling of being an integral part of the larger community—were suddenly gone. The insult was immense, especially to Abu Talib. Drawing a shawl over his shoulders, he stood outside his new home and looked on at his people, sadness coming to dwell in his old, tired eyes.

The track leading to the Valley of Shi'b was quiet, except for the gentle clip-clop of a donkey tugged along in the early morning light by a servant boy with a mission. Whenever the opportunity arose, some kind souls from Quraysh would smuggle supplies into the valley. The servant shivered as he neared the encampment, overshadowed by the mighty mountain range on the outskirt of Makkah.

"And where do you think you're going?" Abu Jahl called out from atop his dark steed, galloping ferociously towards the boy. He spotted the bag of flour amongst other provisions contained in the wicker basket and growled. "I swear by God, I will kill your family to the last man if you go any further."

There was no need for chase, for the boy collapsed onto his knees before the horse had even stopped. "I'm ... I'm only fo-fo-following my master's orders, my chief."

Before Abu Jahl could reach for his whip, a passer-by intervened. "Are you trying to prevent him from taking food to starving children? Let him go, you cruel man!"

"You have forsaken the ways of your fathers who were better than you," Abu Jahl replied, peering down with a look of disgust at the man.

Abu Jahl was well aware that some of the other tribes grew increasingly uneasy about the boycott, which had now lasted for two and half years. On most nights, the wailing of starving children echoed off the nearby mountains, cries that played on the conscience of many inside Makkah. He decided to let the servant boy be—at least this time—and sharply turned his horse in a way that the tip of its tail flicked the intervener's face. The man waved his hand in an abrupt gesture before sending the nervous servant to complete his task.

The items of food, although few, were greatly appreciated as the people had resorted to boiling leaves and shrubs to contain their hunger. Despite the gruelling condition and constant hardship, the Prophet remained undeterred. By day, the Prophet would do everything in his power to strengthen their resolve, imploring them that if they were patient and placed their trust in Allah, then success would be theirs. As they were moved further and further to the verge of despair, he would often describe Paradise to give their struggle meaning and instil in them hope of a better future.

"It has delights which no eye has seen, and beauty the likes of which no ear has heard, things that no human mind has ever imagined,"[29] he would say as they listened on with hopeful hearts.

Day after day as the years went by, Prophet Muhammad continued to check in on everybody, whether followers or fellow tribespeople, to assist and console them. Even though he was often at the brink of starvation himself, he kept his suffering quiet for the sake of being a pillar of strength. Only Allah knew the extent of his suffering, and only Allah's consolation strengthened his spirits. During this period of hardship, the Prophet was counselled and consoled by the words of Allah through Revelation that at times sounded almost like that of a protective parent:

> *By the grace of your Lord, you O Prophet are not insane.*
> *You will certainly have a never-ending reward. And you*
> *are truly a man of outstanding character.*

[Qur'an 68: 4]

§

It had taken nearly three years for the Quraysh leadership to acknowledge the growing calls to end the boycott by the other tribes, but it took five brave men to finally end it: Abul Bukhtari—the passer-by who had saved the servant boy from the clutches of Abu Jahl—as well as Mut'im, Zuhayr, Hisham, and Zam'ah. None of them were Muslim, but they shared a sense of justice and fairness that stopped them from being passive in the face of cruelty. Hisham came up with an ingenious idea to end the ban.

One day, they approached the Ka'bah while Abu Jahl and his comrades rested in the shade. They avoided exchanging looks and pretended as though each had come on their own accord. After the traditional seven circuits around the Ka'bah, Zuhayr raised his voice in a public appeal: "O people of Makkah! How can we live as we are when some of our relatives are starving and dying?"

A few people paused in their activity.

"He is right! End the boycott!" exclaimed Zam'ah, his words causing earnest murmurs. "This merciless siege has gone on for long enough!"

People huddled closer to listen, forming a sizeable crowd. Abu Jahl tried to shut it down, dismissively waving his hands. "This was agreed by all the tribes."

"We do not agree with what our brothers and sisters have had to endure," Mut'im said from the side. "And we will not give up until this pact is destroyed!"

Abu Jahl scoffed.

"He is correct." Abul Bukhtari stepped in. "This is not what we signed up for. The boycott was never meant to hurt *every* member of those tribes, and certainly not to this extent."

It was Hisham's turn. He nodded vehemently in agreement, coaxing the crowd to join in. "Indeed! We do not support this, do we?"

It was a well-thought-out plan, and it was working. Others began to chime in, and soon the chant of "END THE BOYCOTT! END THE BOYCOTT!" could be heard throughout the sanctuary.

Abu Jahl beckoned for his men and they gathered around; he was far too stubborn to concede to these sudden concerns. Two groups quickly formed in front of the Ka'bah and began eyeing each other. Before things could turn ugly, Abu Talib, who had been sitting quietly in a corner all along, stood up. He slowly walked towards the crowd, his trademark ivory robe now faded with patchwork. Still, he made for a distinguished figure and the commotion settled when he spoke.

"O Quraysh! Look at the parchment upon which these unjust laws have been written. Muhammad has revealed that termites have eaten every piece except for the name of God. If this claim turns out to be false, then I shall no longer stand between you and Muhammad. However, if he has spoken the truth, then the boycott must end now."

Those who were for the boycott sneered, accepting this seemingly foolish challenge. Eagerly, Mu'tim and his group rushed closer to the Ka'bah.

They were quickly followed by Abu Jahl and his crowd close on their heels. The only words still legible on the tattered parchment were the customary opening ones:

"Bismik-Allahumma

In Your Name, O Allah"

Abu Talib quickly sought out his nephew and grabbed him in a tight embrace. "It is as you said, my nephew!"

Muhammad smiled gently into his uncle's shoulder. His heart was filled with gratefulness to his Creator. Perhaps, Abu Talib would recognize this sign, how the tiniest of creatures tore apart the most stubborn of pacts formed by those with the hardest hearts. Perhaps his uncle would reflect on the timing of it all, that five men had built the courage to call for justice, and that miraculously not even a fight was required to end the seemingly never-ending siege.

At long last, tents were pulled down and mules were loaded to transport belongings back into Makkah. Prophet Muhammad stood beside his dear wife and children as they gave one last look at the valley, their hearts and tongues alive with the whisper of "*Alhamdulillah!* All praise be to Allah."

Chapter 11
Year of Sadness

It happened so suddenly. There was no long illness to forewarn; it could have been brought about by the trauma of living through the lengthy boycott or simply the fact that she was in her sixties, a good old age for someone living in the seventh century. In the tenth year of her husband's prophethood, Khadijah, known as the Mother of the Believers, passed away. Prophet Muhammad, now nearing fifty, was visibly shaken by the loss. It had been in her arms that he had sought shelter after that terrifying night coming home from the Cave of Hira. It was her voice that had reassured him. Khadijah had spent selflessly in support of his Message. Together they had faced hardship, ridicule, and violence, persevering through it all. And now, just when it seemed there might again be some measure of peace for them, she was gone, and he was utterly bereft.

The two had lived together in harmony for twenty-five years. Khadijah had been not only his wife but also his intimate friend, wise counsellor, and mother to his whole household, including Ali and Zayd. In the wake of her passing, the Prophet began spending more time at home. Home was where warm memories still lingered. Here, the Prophet took comfort surrounded by the belongings of his beloved wife, yet her absence was felt in full force whenever he would return home, knowing hers would not be among the voices returning his greeting.

His daughters were overcome with grief. The Prophet comforted them by telling them about when Jibril had once told him to give Khadijah greetings of Peace from her Lord and to tell her that He had prepared for her a wondrous palace in Paradise. This knowledge helped soothe the painful ache in their hearts whenever they missed their dear mother.

While the Prophet was still reeling from Khadijah's death, Abu Talib fell ill and never recovered. One evening as the velvet blanket of the night fell upon Makkah, Muhammad left for his uncle's home. The lamp lights flickered as the door shut behind him, wisps of cool air evaporating into the chamber where Abu Talib lay upon his bed. He appeared fragile with old age, gentle wrinkles crawling from his forehead to his cheeks which twitched with a slight smile upon hearing his nephew's voice.

Muhammad sat by his bedside, clutching on to his uncle's weakened hand. Ever since he was a boy, Abu Talib had been the Prophet's guardian, putting himself and his reputation on the line when people turned against his nephew. Aware of his uncle's many sacrifices, the Prophet was intent on saving him, and so he called him once more to the worship of the one Creator. As life began to fade from his eyes, Muhammad gently urged, "Say it, uncle. *Laa ilaaha illa Allah*. Just say this one word and I shall be able to stand as a witness for you on the Day of Judgment..."

Abu Talib blinked his tired eyes. Slowly turning his face towards his nephew, he tightened his grip as if to show agreement. Then his lips parted, "My dearest nephew. You know I do believe that—"

A sharp clap interrupted the solemn moment. They were not alone. Abu Jahl was sitting at the back of the room with a comrade also wanting to share some last words with the elderly nobleman.

"By God! If your father were here right now..." said Abu Jahl, shaking his head. "Are you really going to turn your back on the way of Abdul Muttalib now? Discard the religion of your father?"

Abu Talib turned his face away from his nephew, letting out a weary sigh. The Prophet continued to plead, now more emotional than before as the hour of death drew near. Likewise, the Quraysh leaders persisted with reminders of his ancestors, their prestige and traditions.

Abu Talib's last words came out in a low voice. "Were it not that they would consider this dishonourable and say that I was afraid of death, I would say it if only to give you pleasure, my nephew. But I must persist on the way of my father."[30]

The Prophet's heart sank in disappointment. And just like that, within a few weeks of each other, Khadijah and Abu Talib were both gone. Although he knew that every soul must return to Allah, he was human after all, and the loss hit hard.

It took Revelation from the Heavens to console his grieving heart:

> *You surely cannot guide whoever you like O Prophet, it is
> God who guides whoever He wills: He knows best those
> who will follow guidance.*

[Qur'an 28: 56]

The Almighty had decreed in His wisdom that Muhammad's two main
bastions of support—one driven by love, the other by loyalty—would no
longer be by his side. With Abu Talib gone, the dynamics shifted. The
Hashim Tribe needed to select a new chief, and their choice did not bode
well for Muhammad. Though they had not ousted Abu Talib during the
boycott as his half-brother Abu Lahab had hoped, they now considered
this man with a temperament as fiery as his red complexion for the
task. Thus, the "father of flame" was the next in line, replacing Prophet
Muhammad's protector with one of his staunchest opponents.

Keeping with tradition, Abu Lahab as the new chief of the Hashim Tribe
pledged his protection to all tribe members—but the protection offered to
Muhammad was a complete sham. The Prophet was ill-treated like never
before. On one occasion, a passer-by noticed Muhammad was sitting in
his courtyard and leaned over, tossing sheep's intestines, splattering him
with blood and gore. Before disposing of it, the Prophet picked up the
entrails on the end of a stick and while standing at his gate, he called out:
"My fellow tribesmen! What kind of protection do you call this?"[31]

The people kept their eyes downcast, pretending not to see or hear.

Another day, as the Prophet was coming from the Ka'bah, a man took a
handful of dirt, throwing it in his face and over his head. His usually dark
hair was ashen, his beard and shoulders matted in clay-coloured dust and
grime. When he returned home one of his daughters saw him. She burst
into tears at the attempts at degrading and humiliating her father. It was
painful to see. Still, he carried himself with quiet dignity through it all.
Trying to console her, the Prophet said, "Dear daughter, do not cry, for
Allah will protect your father!"

His voice held no uncertainty, and as he wiped away her tears with his
thumb, his daughter's gaze met his. His eyes held no uncertainty too.

The Prophet realized he needed to act quickly and find the means to
protect his family and followers who he so deeply cared for. He decided
to seek support outside of Makkah, a drastic move as it could easily be

spun by the Quraysh chiefs as an act of treachery towards the entire community of Makkah.

The sun, a golden coin in the sky, rose high over two cloaked figures as they navigated the dunes. The hot sand shimmered beneath the glaring rays as the Prophet made his way on foot to Ta'if, about thirty miles east of Makkah, travelling with his former slave, Zayd the son of Haritha. Along the way, he invited each tribe they encountered to embrace Islam.

Finally, they reached Ta'if. The fragrance of honey wafted in the wind like a pleasant welcome. The Prophet passed through the city walls and walked by the attractive gardens, orchards, and cornfields, heading straight to meet three brothers, chieftains of the Thaqif Tribe. The atmosphere was chilling, and his invitation to accept Islam was met with a cold reception.

"If you were sent by God as you claim, then your status is too lofty for the likes of me to speak with you," came one sarcastic response to his plea. "And if you are taking the name of God in vain, then it's not fit that I should speak with you."

Another chief looked down at him and scoffed, "Couldn't God have sent someone better than you?"

Disheartened by their arrogant mockery, the Prophet left them. It was obvious that they would not offer their protection, and so he turned his focus elsewhere. In the days that followed, he called to the townspeople, young and old, servants and nobility, inviting them to Islam. No one appeared interested.

Amongst the places he preached was the marketplace, the centre of activity in any city. Children ran by, climbing over low walls and hopping over baskets, disturbing the elderly who huddled together to swap stories. Merchants captivated passers-by with sweet bargains as servants carried vessels overflowing with the renowned figs and glistening red pomegranates of the region. Tai'f stood out amidst the valleys and mountains in the otherwise arid area. The Prophet had hoped that the people's hearts were as fertile as the land, but soon their true nature became clear.

Annoyed by his continued presence, the chiefs made plans to get rid of him. "Gather the riff-raff, slaves and the wayward children," they commanded. "Make sure those two are driven out of this city, even if you need to use force."

The chiefs turned the people against the Prophet, who they framed as an unwanted guest. The townspeople's apathy towards him instantly turned to enmity. "Away with you!" they shouted, forming a sizeable crowd as they hurled harsh words at the two surprised men. "Go back to where you came from!"

A stone hit the Prophet's forehead. Shocked, he turned to see where it came from. His gaze met that of a little boy who grinned as he picked up another pebble. It seemed as though even the children had been ordered to harass them. In a matter of minutes, the environment became as hostile as Makkah, and so the Prophet decided it was best to leave. The insults from the crowd showed that little progress was possible at this point. Zayd started using his own body as a shield to protect the Prophet as more stones burst forth, his head receiving multiple cuts in the process. Soon, the people gave chase, their feet rapidly crossing the marketplace, the alleys, and the pathway out of the city as they relentlessly pelted the two with stones.

By the time they outran the mob, blood trickled down the Prophet's calves, soaking his sandals. A fair distance away from the city, they sank into the shade of a nearby orchard to catch their breath. Vines as thick as snakes trailed down the wall the Prophet leaned on. Briefly, he closed his eyes, body covered with injuries. Khadijah's loving support was now painfully absent. He then rose to his knees, lifting his arms—battered and bruised from the onslaught—to the sky as he cried out:

> *"O Allah! I complain to You of my weakness and dishonour before people. You are the Most Merciful, the Lord of the weak and my Lord too. To whom have you entrusted me? To one who does not care for me? Or have you appointed my enemy as master of my affairs? So long as You are not angry with me, I care not. Your favour is abundant for me. I seek refuge in the light of Your Face, by which all darkness is dispelled and every affair of this world and the next is set right, in case Your anger or Your displeasure descend upon me. All I desire is Your pleasure and satisfaction. There is no power and no might except in You."[32]*

The time in Ta'if was one of the most painful moments in the Prophet's life, firmly etched into his memory such that he would later recall it as the hardest day in his life. Yet, he endured this unwarranted onslaught with patience. This supplication, known as the Prayer of the Oppressed or *Du'a al-Mustad'afeen*, was a heartfelt moment in which he sought connection with his Creator. As long as Allah was pleased with him, the hardships were bearable. Allah's pleasure meant more to the Prophet than the acceptance and favour of the people.

Resting against the wall, the Prophet took in the sweet scent of the gardens nearby, unaware that he was being closely watched. The owners of the orchard were two brothers, Utbah and Shaybah, who were visiting from Makkah. Sympathy tugged their hearts when they saw the condition he was in. Quickly, they called for their servant.

"Take these grapes to Muhammad."

Addas walked in short, brisk strides until he reached the Prophet. He presented the tray of grapes, hues of purple and red making for an attractive sight. The Prophet, who stood up upon his approach, gladly accepted the offering. As he brought one plump grape to his mouth, he said, "*Bismillah*, in the name of God."

Addas was taken aback. "By God, the people in this land do not utter such words," he remarked.

Realizing that this man was a foreigner, the Prophet then asked, "Where are you from and what is your religion?"

"I am a Christian from Nineveh in Iraq."

The Prophet dipped his head in a nod. "So you are from the town of a righteous man, Jonah (Yunus), son of Matta."

This shocked Addas down to the core. The tray slightly quivered in his hand. He asked, "How do you know about him?"

"He was my brother," the Prophet replied, explaining, "He was a prophet and I am a prophet."

The Prophet then recited a few verses about Prophet Jonah. Addas was as overwhelmed as he was impressed. He fell to his knees, kissing the Prophet's feet in a gesture of respect as was common back home. Muhammad now felt less isolated, seeing the encounter with Addas as a reminder of all the people in the vast world beyond Arabia who would understand his message, even if his own would not.

When Addas returned to Utbah and Shaybah, they wasted no time reprimanding him. "What is the matter with you? Why on earth did you fall on your face and kiss his feet, who told you to do this?!"

He explained, "O my masters! There is none better than him on this earth." His eyes glistened in excitement. "He told me something that none but a prophet could know."

Addas knew without a doubt that this was a true Prophet of God, and so he accepted the call to Islam, much to his masters' contempt. Their initial sympathy morphed into regret that they had sent him.

As soon as they regained enough strength, the Prophet and Zayd continued on the journey home. Along the way, a mysterious cloud appeared in the previously clear blue sky. The Prophet looked up to see that Allah had sent Jibril and the Angel of Mountains. They had come to show their support.

"Peace be upon you," said the Angel of Mountains. "If you so wish, I will lift two mountains and crush the entire city for you."

The Prophet immediately understood that the Almighty was responding to his prayers. He now had a chance to seek vengeance against those who harmed him. Where most would have relished the opportunity, the Prophet declined. "I hope that Allah will raise from among their descendants people who will worship Allah as One, and will not set up partners with Him," he told the angels.

Feeling content that Allah was pleased with him and his efforts, the Prophet shrugged off the adversity of Ta'if and set his sights on Makkah with a renewed drive. When the outline of the city appeared on the horizon, the Prophet and Zayd set up camp. It was unsafe for the Prophet to proceed any further without first securing the protection of a tribe leader, so he sent word to several. None agreed to help, some outright refusing while others offered feeble excuses.

Finally, a nobleman offered his protection. It was Mut'im, a man amongst the few who petitioned against the boycott two years earlier. He sent a small group of fully-armed men to accompany Muhammad back into the city and directly to the sanctuary of the Ka'bah for all to see. This was a favour the Prophet would never forget.

After the Prophet made the customary circuits around the Ka'bah, Mut'im announced to the Quraysh, "I have extended my protection to Muhammad."

Abu Sufyan, decked in elegant shades of red and mustard, stepped forward. With sharp eyes, he asked the aging man, "Have you joined his religion?"

Mut'im stood firm, his weathered gaze not faltering for a second. "I am only giving him my protection."

With a calculating gaze, Abu Sufyan thought for a moment before turning. "If that is the case, we will accept your protection."

For now... he added silently.

Chapter 12
The End of Knowledge

The night was still. Peaceful quiet filled the empty twists and turns of the streets, the inhabitants of Makkah subdued by sleep. The Prophet had also been fast asleep, recuperating after a night of solemn prayer, until Jibril made his presence known. The air shifted with a sense of urgency as the angel instructed him to wake up.

The coolness of the evening surrounded the Ka'bah. Shadows cast by the pale moon dappled upon the stone ground, undisturbed except for the slight movement of the Prophet, who stood by the Hijr. From this semi-circular wall near the Ka'bah, he was close to the spot where his grandfather Abdul Muttalib used to rest—a time that seemed so far away. Jibril placed his hand on Muhammad's back as a heavenly creature came forward, hooves gently thudding against the stone slab below.

"This is Buraq." Jibril's voice was reassuring.

The animal was unlike any creature known to man. It was medium in size, smaller than a mule but bigger than a donkey. Its pearly white coat shimmered in the silvery moonlight. Just as the Prophet was about to mount the creature, it pulled back, shying away from him.

"Of all people! Will you behave like this with Muhammad?" remarked Jibril.

The creature remained withdrawn until Jibril revealed to it that Muhammad was the leader of all prophets and the best of creation. "Just know that no one more honourable than he has ridden you."

At this, Buraq began to sweat intensely. The majestic creature inched forward and lowered itself into a humble kneel. The Prophet mounted Buraq, and in the company of Jibril, they set forth following the North Star on a journey known as *Israa*. Buraq took off at a miraculous speed, each stride launching it as far as the eye could see.[33] With a rush of cool air, distant lands rolled by in a mesmerizing display. They sped past

Yathrib and beyond Khaybar. With each leap, the pain and difficulty from the Year of Sadness became more distant as they speared through the night towards Jerusalem, the same direction the Prophet and his followers turned to when praying.

When they reached the blessed lands, the Prophet noticed the mounts tied outside the Sacred Mosque of Worship. Al-Aqsa was a landmark of religious significance. The structure stood solidly, its ancient architecture a testament to its rich history. The Prophet tied Buraq to a post before stepping inside, where he found all the previous Prophets waiting for him, the chamber appearing spacious yet also filled to capacity. These were his brothers, part of the prophetic family—all connected by the same purpose, chosen to convey the same message. They gestured him forward with nods of respect and admiration. He soon found himself front and centre, the men quickly moving to form straight rows behind him.

With Abraham, Moses, and Jesus standing over his shoulder, Prophet Muhammad sensed that this moment represented a turning point. Leading this congregation in this blessed space served as a sign—the orphan from the desert of Arabia had become the leader of all the Prophets humanity had ever seen. His role extended beyond that of tribes, race, and in that moment, even time, for it became clearer than ever as he led them in prayer that he was the seal, the Final Prophet. The responsibility of conveying the final message rested on his shoulders, and the honour of leading the noble Prophets in prayer was his.

Prophet Muhammad raised his hands to lead them all in prayer. "*Allahu akbar...*" Allah is Greater.

After this extraordinary experience, he followed Jibril. The Archangel placed three vessels in front of the Prophet, one filled with wine, the other with milk, and the third with honey. The Prophet took a moment to look at them. He had never drunk wine before, even though the Makkans loved it. The delicately creamy milk contrasted against the syrupy amber gleam of the honey. From these options, he chose the second vessel. He brought it to his mouth and drank from it.

"You chose milk due to the purity of your nature," said Jibril. Muhammad began to smile as the Archangel continued, "Hence you have received guidance and your followers have too."

Jibril further explained, "Had you chosen the wine, your followers would have been astray."

The Prophet felt a deep sense of relief and gratitude enter his heart. His nation would follow the middle way, the path that steered far away from extremism.

An enchanting ladder was then brought forward.[34] The Prophet stared at it in amazement. The stars twinkled alongside the astonishing object that pierced the sky. It spiralled upwards almost unendingly. Jibril gestured for the Prophet to proceed forward, reassuring him that this was all for him and that he would be by his side throughout the journey. Muhammad took the first step, and onwards they both went, beyond the realm of this world, ascending into the Heavens. This ascending journey would be known as *Mi'raj.*

As the Prophet looked back at Jibril, he saw the Archangel transform into his true form, six-hundred wings now stretching open. His unfurling wings seemed to fill the horizons as the world faded behind them. Each time his feathers rustled, the Prophet saw precious stones such as rubies and pearls falling from them. Unbeknownst to Prophet Muhammad, he would soon have the opportunity to reunite with the Prophets he had prayed with in Jerusalem, though no longer in the forms they had been in during their earthly life. He would find them coming to greet him in their celestial forms, a sight that would amaze him. But before that, he had to pass through the gates of the first Heaven.

When they arrived at the gates, Jibril called out to the gatekeeper and requested it to be opened. The gatekeeper asked, "Who is it?"

The Archangel answered, "It is Jibril."

"Who accompanies you?"

"Muhammad."

"Has he been called?" asked the gatekeeper, to which Jibril replied in the affirmative. Immediately, the gates of the nearest Heaven opened wide. "He is welcome, and what a wonderful visitor he is!" the gatekeeper expressed in joy.

In the first Heaven, Prophet Adam, the father of mankind, stepped forward to welcome them. He greeted the Prophet warmly, "Peace be upon you."

"And upon you be peace," Muhammad replied, the final Prophet standing face to face with the first human being, the first Prophet.

Adam declared that indeed Muhammad was the Prophet of Allah. The Prophet then noticed two groups of people. The group on the right—believers—brought a smile on Adam's face, but when looking to the people on the left, Adam wept. Prophet Muhammad realized that the second group was the disbelievers.

Countless angels flocked to greet Muhammad as he passed through the first Heaven. The experience was joyful and warm. Among them was Malik, the Warden of Hell, who never smiles. Malik showed the Prophet a view of Hell and the terrible plight of those languishing therein. He saw people behaving as man-eating beasts, devouring human corpses—a fitting punishment for backbiting. The wild look of desperation in their eyes was permanently etched in his memory. It was a fate no one would wish for.

They reached the second Heaven, where Jibril once again asked for the gate to be opened. Beyond the gates were the two cousins, Prophets John (Yahya) and Jesus. Greetings of peace were exchanged before they acknowledged Muhammad's prophethood just as Adam had.[35] The Prophet left for the third Heaven where he met Joseph, whose beauty struck him, for he was more radiant than the full moon. Like the others, Joseph also acknowledged Muhammad as Allah's final Prophet. Once at the fourth Heaven, Enoch (Idris) was there to receive him, their dialogue ending with the past Prophet expressing his faith in Muhammad as the Last Messenger. The same occurred at the fifth Heaven, where Aaron (Harun) came forward with heartfelt salutations. Each interaction, although brief, strengthened Muhammad's resolve in his role, the flame of determination coaxed brighter.

They moved on. The gates of the sixth Heaven opened to reveal Moses, the Prophet who had the honour of hearing Allah speak, the one who stood up and opposed the worst of all tyrants, Pharaoh. Moses offered his greetings before testifying that Muhammad was indeed a Prophet. As Jibril gestured for Muhammad to proceed to the next Heaven, Moses began to weep.

The Prophet paused in his step, then gently asked, "What makes you cry?"

"The reason for my tears is that someone much younger was sent as a Prophet after me, and yet his followers will enter Paradise in greater numbers than mine," Moses said.

Up until that moment, Moses had had the largest following of believers. His words rang in the Prophet's mind as he reunited with Jibril and journeyed upward. Upon reaching the seventh level of the Heavens, the Prophet saw Abraham leaning against *Bait Al-Ma'mur*, the heavenly equivalent of the Ka'bah on Earth. It was amazing to find that Prophet Abraham, who had built the Ka'bah many centuries ago, was resting near its equivalent in the Heavens. Jibril explained that a group of 70,000 different angels visited every day to circuit around this holy structure, and upon finishing, a new group of 70,000 angels would arrive.

The Prophet stepped forward to exchange greetings with his forefather, who then also testified that Muhammad was the Prophet of Allah.

The events of the night were but a glimpse at the Almighty's limitless power. Prophet Muhammad was in awe. The lightning-fast Buraq. Ascending the Heavens and seeing glimpses of the Afterlife. Meeting the Prophets, the concept of time and space no longer a barrier. The seemingly impossible was possible for Allah. All these were signs shown to the Prophet for a reason. His heart beat faster in anticipation of what awaited beyond *Sidrat al-Muntaha*, a majestic tree where Jibril came to a halt. The Archangel announced that he was unable to go any further—in fact, no creature had moved beyond this point. The beautiful lote tree with leaves the size of elephant ears and fruits the size of pitchers represented the end of all knowledge. What lay beyond was known only to the Creator, and Muhammad had the sole privilege to step into that realm.

Prophet Muhammad progressed beyond the tree until he met with Allah. Although there was now nothing between him and the Lord of all the Worlds, the intensity of the Divine Light made it impossible for him to gaze upon the Most Merciful. Allah addressed him and gifted him fifty daily prayers that would allow his followers to stay connected to their Creator throughout the day and night. Although some form of prayer already existed, *salah* was now officially obligatory as a fixed daily number. The Prophet immediately recognized the immense value of these prescribed prayers—compared to all other commandments, *salah* was not conveyed to him while on the earth, rather he was elevated to the Heavens to receive it. It was the only order that Allah directly conveyed.

With this valuable commandment to share with his followers, he reunited with Jibril and they began their descent. On his way back, Moses stopped him.

"What did Allah command you?"

"Fifty prayers a day for my nation," he replied.

"Your followers will not be able to manage that," Moses said. Through his own experience with the Children of Isra'il, he knew that such an instruction would be a crushing burden for most people. "Go back to your Lord and ask Him to lessen it for you."

Taking Moses' advice, the Prophet returned to the Almighty. Out of His mercy, Allah decreased the number of obligatory prayers. When the Prophet passed by, Moses stopped him again.

"What happened?"

"It was reduced to forty."

Moses advised the Prophet to ask for it to be reduced further. And so, the Prophet returned. Moses stopped him once more, only to find out that the prayers had been lessened to thirty. He dipped his head slightly and then advised the Prophet to go back. Thirty became twenty, and twenty became ten. This exchange went on, the Prophet going back and forth until the original fifty became five daily prayers.

When Moses heard the amount, he advised the Prophet to request to lighten the prayers once again. Speaking from his experience, he said, "The Children of Isra'il were asked to do less but still were unable to."

But the Prophet could not bear the thought of going back again. "I feel too shy before my Lord to go back to Him."

Then, a voice announced: "I have established My obligation and lightened it for My servants. He who prays these five prayers will be rewarded as if he had prayed fifty. What I decree cannot be changed."[36]

The sense of finality was evident. Although only five prayers were obliged, the reward would be that of fifty—on top of that, performing prayers was a way for believers to draw near to the Creator, to nourish their souls and strengthen their spirituality. The Prophet recognized this as a gift for those who truly believe.

The time had arrived for the Prophet to return home. He descended the Heavens with Jibril, his spirits lifted and his mind focused on the mission of fulfilling and conveying this significant commandment. Riding Buraq, he returned to Makkah before dawn with newfound conviction and the sense of a new beginning. Soon enough, the freshly-risen sun cast a soft golden glow across the desert landscape. As the early-morning activity began to pick up, the Prophet wasted no time. He set out and began to speak to some people, sharing the story of his Miraculous Journey.

The news travelled like wildfire. It soon reached Abu Jahl and his comrades. "This is patently RIDICULOUS!" they crowed, some of them in grave danger of laughing themselves to death.

"Every child knows that a caravan takes a month to go to Syria and a month to return, and Muhammad claims he made the journey to Jerusalem and back in one night?" the Quraysh scoffed.

His opponents, filled with poisonous glee, called everyone to come to listen to the story for themselves. They laughed, clapped, and howled. As always, they were eager to mock, grasping this opportunity with greedy hands. Those who had been to Jerusalem asked specific questions, trying to catch him out, but the Prophet patiently responded with detailed answers that only someone who had visited Jerusalem would know. Still, they found it all ludicrous, unmoved by the fact that Muhammad was, in fact, as sincere as he was right.

While some remained behind to slyly quiz the Prophet further, the rest ran to where Abu Bakr was. They sought to convey this tale to the Prophet's dearest friend in hopes of rocking his faith and looked forward to relishing his expression as it happened.

"Abu Bakr, O Abu Bakr!" they called before letting the seemingly absurd story spill forth.

"So there! What do you have to say about Muhammad now?"

There was barely a pause before Abu Bakr answered, "*If* he said that, then it must be the truth."

Abu Jahl's right eye began twitching. The certainty in Abu Bakr's response had caught them all off guard and their laughs began to wane.

"And what is so strange about that anyway?" Abu Bakr continued, finding no issue with the Miraculous Journey they had tried to discredit. Their hopes plummeted with each word his calm and steady voice imparted. "In fact, I believe in something even more bewildering: that an angel descends on him bearing news from the Heavens."

Abu Bakr's faith in Allah and His Messenger proved unshakable. From that day onward, he earned the title of *Siddiq*—someone willing to stand with the truth no matter the consequences. Wordlessly, they retreated, mouths twisted in disappointment, unaware that the man they left in their wake would one day become their leader—and indeed the leader of the whole of Arabia—in only a matter of years.

§

The Prophet's *"Israa"* is mentioned in the Qur'an in the following verse:

> *"Glory to Allah Who took His slave on a journey by night from the Sacred Mosque to the Farthest Mosque whose precincts I did bless, in order that I might show him some of My signs. Verily, Allah hears and sees all things."*

[Qur'an 17: 1]

Chapter 13
A Beacon of Hope

The season of pilgrimage bustled with people gathering from far and wide, pilgrims pitching their tents and merchants pulling their carts to the open areas where they would set up stalls for the festivals.

During the Days of Sacrifice, the Prophet went to the valley of Mina, where the pilgrims would camp for three days. Over the years, he would visit the tribes on pilgrimage coming from across the Arabian Peninsula, declaring his message and reciting Qur'an to whoever would lend an ear. On one such occasion, beneath the blanket of darkness and stars dotting the night sky, he had come across six men from Yathrib—the pre-Islamic name for the city of Madinah. They had heard of his supposed prophethood, and as soon as he told them who he was, their faces had lit up. This was the man they had been hearing of!

"We came to know of you many years ago," one of the men had said while placing his hand over the shoulders of his fellow tribesmen. The Prophet appeared intrigued by this, and so he continued, "You see, the Jewish Tribes living alongside us constantly taunt us. 'A Prophet is now about to be sent' they say. 'We will follow him, and we will slay you as 'Ad and 'Iram were slain.'" They were referring to two ancient nations that had been wiped out.

An amused look, followed by a modest smile appeared on Muhammad's face. ...If only the Jewish Tribes would accept him that easily, he thought to himself.

Motivated by the Prophet's attentiveness, one of the younger men called Raafi' spoke up. "We are especially intrigued," he began, "by the way the Quraysh so adamantly vilified a man they had once unanimously respected as *al-Amin*, the trustworthy."

The Prophet simply smiled in response, his silence exuding dignity. While most would have rushed to speak harsh words about their opponents, the Prophet was not that way inclined and instead asked if he could stay and speak with them more openly. The men readily made room for him, welcoming his presence.

"Please sit," they had said, and he settled amongst them, crossed-legged on the ground. The way he carried himself, an admirable blend of nobility and humility, greatly contrasted the rumours the Quraysh had circulated to the pilgrims.

A short distance away, a lizard skittered across the plain, retreating beneath a rock in search of warmth. One of the men stoked the crackling campfire with a stick as the rest turned to the Prophet, some of them leaning forward expectantly.

"Tell me more about yourselves," the Prophet asked, wanting to become better acquainted with this modest audience.

"We are from the Khazraj Tribe, from the city of Yathrib."

Muhammad nodded. He was no stranger to Yathrib, having visited the oasis town to meet the distant relatives from his late mother's side when he was a child. Abu Bakr had already informed him that the city was entangled in inter-tribal rivalry over issues of land ownership between the two largest tribes: the Khazraj and the Aws. One group would raid on enemy territory in typical barbaric fashion, which then had to be avenged, and gradually they became caught up in a cycle of violence. The constant warfare was ruining their land. The ordinary people were exhausted by the conflicts and were now desperately seeking a leader to unite them.

The Prophet listened as they introduced themselves. Unlike many, these six men appeared genuinely interested to hear him out. Now that acquaintances had been made, the Prophet proceeded to give them sincere counsel, explaining the message of Islam with great passion. The group of men absorbed everything he had to say, eyes eager and ears keen to listen. They appreciated the way he turned fully towards whoever he was addressing. It made them feel honoured, as though they were guests in his home, when in fact they were but strangers in a valley lit up by scattered campfires.

The men were as equally impressed by his manners as they were by the purity of his message. Realizing that he fit the description of the Prophet long awaited for by the Jewish Tribes in Yathrib, they said to themselves: "Let us pledge our allegiance to him before they do!"

Having grown up amidst Jewish Tribes, the concept of monotheism and scripture was familiar to them, and the divinity of the Qur'an was undeniable to this group of six men. As the Prophet continued to speak about the beauty of Islam, he expressed his intention to live amongst them under their protection. The men quickly realized that this religion, with the backing of a Prophet, had the power to deliver peace and prosperity to their troubled souls. It could put an end to the petty feuds that had plagued their people for so long. They had only a few questions, which the Prophet dutifully answered before they declared their faith.

Before having to return to their city, the new converts wanted to give a clear picture of the political and social situation to the Prophet and reassure him of their commitment. "We have given up on our people, for we are being torn apart by civil war! And it may just be that Allah will unite us through *you*," they expressed earnestly. Despite having spent a short time in his company, they recognized in him the qualities of a just leader, which is exactly what they needed after losing most of their leadership in the most recent carnage of Yathrib's spiralling feuds.

"We will return and invite the people to your religion so that they may accept it as we have accepted it. If Allah were to unite them around you, then no man will be mightier than you."[37]

The Prophet was delighted by their resolve; he had planted a seed and hoped to see it blossom in the years to come. The men promised to fulfil the conditions of Islam and arranged to meet with him again during the next Hajj season. With a nod, the Prophet agreed and then stood up, greeting each of them before parting ways. As they watched the Prophet leave, a striking figure humbly cloaked in a simple robe, faith surged in their hearts with a warmth that rivalled that of the campfire's dancing flames.

Word reached the Quraysh, but they did not care much for this development. As far as they were concerned, Yathrib was the boondocks—a useful caravan stop, but really just a loose string of villages along the eight miles of a fertile spring-fed valley thick with date palms. Being the centre of religion and trade in Arabia, the people of Makkah considered themselves infinitely superior to what they saw as a bunch of peasants.

Meanwhile, the new converts returned home, discreetly spreading news of the Prophet and his pure teachings. They spoke about him enthusiastically as the days flew by until the arrival of the next pilgrimage in the early summer of the year 621. As the sun went down, they ventured to the rendezvous point. To meet inside the city of Makkah would have been unwise, given the level of Quraysh harassment, so the group of Muslims from Yathrib met with Muhammad three miles outside the city.

They gathered in the wide valley of Mina in a spot known as Aqabah. This time there were twelve of them, including two from the Aws Tribe—a promising sign. If even a few Aws and Khazraj could come together under the banner of Islam, perhaps many more could. Perhaps the warring tribes could finally make peace. Since each of the twelve were notables in Yathrib's society, this was a deputation that held promise and opportunity.

The Prophet conveyed to them the message of Islam and the future he envisioned for the Muslim community should they all live together in their city. The men were captured by his eloquence and sincerity. Change hung in the air as they rose to their feet and came forward. Each of the twelve men clasped Muhammad's hand close, forearm against forearm, and pledged himself as a believer and to respect the Prophet's judgement.

"We gave allegiance to the Messenger that we will not associate others with God, nor steal, nor commit fornication, nor kill our children, nor disobey Muhammad in what is right," one of the men recalled to his wife when he returned home, full of excitement. "If we fulfilled this, Paradise would be ours, and if we committed any of these sins, it was for Allah to punish or forgive us as he pleased."

History would record this as the First Pledge of Aqabah. It gave the new converts a completely different set of values to their previous tribal laws. It taught them that all people had certain undeniable rights that had to be respected whether they were from their tribe or an outsider. The bond of faith was stronger than tribal allegiance, and the old law of the jungle was no longer welcome.

For the first time since the initial Revelation in the Cave of Hira eleven years earlier, Muhammad was acting as more than just a Messenger—he now acted as a leader, assuming the political role that his opponents had feared all along. Slipping seamlessly into this new role, the Prophet decided to send one of his Companions along with the group to educate the people in Yathrib about the teachings of Islam and to help them learn the Qur'an. He hand-picked Mus'ab for this role.

Mus'ab was tall and dashingly handsome, known for his spirit of sacrifice and sharp intellect. He radiated the sort of charismatic, bulletproof confidence usually associated with emperors. Raised in the lap of luxury, he had endured great hardship when accepting Islam, his own mother imprisoning and then boycotting him. Yet nothing diminished his fervour for the religion. Readily accepting his mission, he mounted his horse with a small pouch of provisions and set off into the desert. As he neared Yathrib, he admired the row of date palms leading into the city, which was nestled between the surrounding volcanic hills. He observed the people he passed by, soon realizing that the land was split between the tribes—he would have to tread carefully in this volatile city, where tribal feuds were the norm, not the exception.

Mus'ab was warmly welcomed by Asad, a convert to Islam and a man of good standing. Asad made for a generous host, and the two men put every effort into teaching the locals about the religion. Not a day went by without at least one person becoming Muslim, and soon more and more households of the Khazraj Tribe spoke of Prophet Muhammad.

One day Mus'ab and Asad sat in a garden bordering the Aws territory. The date palms swayed, leaves fanning in the gentle breeze. A child dragged a container of water away from the well, unconcerned by the two men's discussion. However, their meeting was of much concern to Sa'd, a leading figure amongst the Aws Tribe, who noticed the two and promptly sought his cousin.

"Usayd," he called out to his cousin. "Go to those two who have come to misguide the weak and foolish, and forbid them to come near our quarters again. If Asad were not my relative, I would have handled him myself..."

Usayd grabbed his spear and made a beeline for the Muslims, wearing an intimidating scowl. Asad saw him marching over and winced at Mus'ab, eyes widening with concern as he whispered, "Watch out. Here comes the chief's right-hand man."

Mus'ab reassured him with a slight tilt of his head before the shadow of Usayd fell over them.

"What brings you two here?" Usayd's voice was thunderous. "We do not want you around here deceiving our weak and ignorant. If you care for your life, you would do well to keep away!" he warned. The tip of his spear flashed menacingly as if to emphasize his point.

Mus'ab did not react, remaining calm in the face of this aggression like he had seen the Prophet do many times when abuse was hurled his way. "Why not sit and hear what we have to say?" he suggested, tone gentle, mirroring the Prophet in manners and demeanour. "If you like it, you can accept it, and if you dislike it, you can reject it."

Usayd liked both the appearance and the manner of the Prophet's envoy. But he did not let down his guard, observing them carefully as he replied with a blunt, "Fine."

He dug his spear into the ground and sat beside them. As Mus'ab conveyed the teachings of Islam, Usayd's scepticism gradually unravelled. He realized that he agreed with every word, his heart resonating with these principles of justice, charity, and the Oneness of God. "How excellent and beautiful are these words!" he remarked.

When Mus'ab recited some verses from the Qur'an, the power of the words struck Usayd. It broke through all his concerns. His expression shifted, softening. Those who were present could now see Islam in his face. "What should I do if I wish to enter this religion?" he said softly, eyes moist with tears.

They told him how to purify himself and perform the prayer. He washed by the nearby well and purified his garments before returning. Usayd then testified, "There is no god but Allah, and Muhammad is the Messenger of Allah."

He prayed as they instructed him, welcoming the tranquillity that it brought. When he was done, he turned to the men, tilting his head in the direction of Sa'd. "There is a man not too far behind me who, if he were to follow you, then truly Muhammad will be followed without fail by every one of his people."

When Usayd returned to Sa'd, it was obvious that he was a changed man. Sa'd furrowed his eyebrows as Usayd made it his mission to convince him to speak to the two men. Before long, the chieftain also embraced Islam, marking a turning point in the spread of Islam in Yathrib. Sa'd becoming Muslim triggered a domino effect in his community, and Mus'ab's calm character proved effective in winning the hearts of the people.

By the time of the next Hajj in early June 622, the deputation from Yathrib to Muhammad had swelled to seventy-three figures representing its most influential families. The number alone testified to how serious they were. Having heard of the harassment and difficulty suffered by the Prophet and his followers, they sought to invite him to Yathrib with glad tidings of a welcoming community of Muslims. They journeyed to Makkah along with a caravan of pagan tribespeople from Yathrib. The majority of the large group of Muslims belonged to the Aws Tribe and eleven from the Khazraj Tribe. Nasiba and Asma were two women who also formed part of the group.

A secret meeting was arranged late one night after the pilgrimage. While the rest of the idol-worshipping pilgrims slept, the Muslims of Yathrib snuck out individually or in pairs until all seventy-three regrouped at Aqabah, where soon they would join in what would be known as the Second Pledge of Aqabah. The Prophet arrived, joined closely by his uncle Abbas. Although he was not Muslim at the time, he worried for his nephew and felt it was his duty to accompany him to this potentially life-changing meeting. The Muslims of Yathrib stared in awe as they came face to face with the handsome countenance yet simplicity of their esteemed Prophet, a man of medium build, with dark hair contained in a neat turban.

Abbas was the first to speak. "You know of the esteem in which we hold Muhammad. We have ensured his security to the best of our ability. He is honoured amongst his people." His voice was steady, eyes slowly moving from one person to the next, weighing up the assembly's resolve. "If you cannot guarantee his protection in Yathrib, then leave him be in Makkah."

Baraa, the spokesperson of the group, replied in full confidence. "We are willing to offer our loyalty and our lives to the Prophet and will readily pledge our allegiance."

Determination shone in his eyes, and the others nodded, echoing their agreement. Abbas could see that they were serious but was not yet convinced. He looked at Muhammed, who began to speak. The Prophet held their attention by reciting Qur'an before setting out the terms of the oath.

Before Baraa could say a word, he was interrupted by Abbas. "Know well what you are all agreeing to," he said, an edge of caution to his tone. "You are pledging to go to war. Should the call of war be sounded, will you answer?"

There was a sense of danger and of bridges being irreversibly burned that everyone felt now that Abbas reminded them of what the oath could mean in the future. By speaking of impending battle, he tested the depth of their commitment.

Baraa gave a firm nod to reassure him he knew exactly what this meant. He turned to the Prophet. "O Messenger of Allah, we are born warriors and have inherited this from generation to generation." He grasped the Prophet's hand. "I swear by Allah we shall protect you as we protect our families."

The next man stepped forward. He paused, considering his words, before asking, "Tell us what will happen if our possessions are lost, and our nobles are killed ... what can we expect in return?"

"Paradise," replied the Prophet.

That was more than enough to encourage the rest of the group to come forward. "Stretch forth your hand," they said, and then pledged their oaths. "We will worship none but Allah and will never join partners with Him. We will obey Allah and His Messenger. We will spend our wealth in charity. We will advise others to do good and prohibit evil. We will protect the Prophet as we protect our women and children."

Speaking the oath aloud, they felt connected by their faith in an indescribable way. Before parting ways into the night, Asad stepped forward. He lifted the Prophet's hand and called to the gathering, "O people of Yathrib, at long last, we have found the Prophet of Allah."

Their eyes shimmered with emotion. Then, turning to face the Prophet, Asad exclaimed, "We are of you and you are of us. Whoever comes to us of your Companions, or if you come to us yourself, we shall defend you as we defend ourselves."[38]

With that, Muhammad was no longer bound to the Quraysh nor Makkah. He had formally bound himself to Yathrib, and Yathrib to him. In time, this pledge would come to be a beacon of hope for the Muslims of Makkah and a thorn in the side for their oppressors.

Chapter 14
Goodbye Makkah

The Prophet soon began sending his followers to Yathrib to settle. This would be their new home, where they were welcome to establish a new life free from persecution. With their heads hung low, many had to leave under cover of darkness, cautiously navigating the narrow alleyways as though they were criminals.

In the middle of the night, the young would help the frail and elderly carefully manoeuvre through the rocky mountain paths out of sight far beyond the outskirts of their home. It felt very much like they were escaping from prison when, in fact, they were fleeing the very place where they were born and raised. They were forsaking the streets of Makkah where they played as children, abandoning the marketplace where they would gleefully laugh with their friends, and bidding goodbye to the memories of familiar faces that once upon a time looked at them with warmth. Their hearts grieved for the fond memories contained in their homeland that had become too painful to continue living in.

What made matters all the more difficult was that Makkah was the sacred land of the Ka'bah, the land of the Prophet Abraham. Abandoning their ancestral homes felt like giving up a part of who they were, but the Prophet, like a loving father, would gently reassure them. "Allah the Almighty has prepared for you new brothers and new homes which will allow you to experience peace and safety once again."

Although their hearts pained, the Companions were not prepared to let go of their faith. The thirteen years of guidance they received from the Prophet had more than prepared them for this huge sacrifice. They knew that for the message of Islam to spread, it was vital that they established a new foundation elsewhere. And so, without knowing if they would ever return, they left everything behind, only carrying with them essential supplies so that they could travel light on their journey to new beginnings. The great *hijrah*—migration—had begun.

One would think that the more Muslims leaving Makkah, the happier the Quraysh would become, but this was far from true. The enemies of Islam noticed the quiet departure, and the mere thought that these people were going off to find a better life somewhere else made them livid. The likes of Abu Jahl were almost suffocating out of frustration.

"Why are the people of Yathrib supporting Muhammad?" he seethed upon hearing this information, his hand haphazardly searching for something to throw. Abu Jahl's face twisted with rage as he considered what this meant for the Quraysh.

They were losing control, and they knew it.

They also had another increasingly growing fear. Yathrib was en route to Syria, one of the key trading partners for the Makkans. If the Muslims settled in Yathrib, they could easily ambush one of their trade caravans or refuse to grant them safe passage. This would be a huge financial blow and an even greater embarrassment to the Quraysh.

Contrary to what they may have thought, these were not easy times for Prophet Muhammad. As more of his followers migrated, the less protection he had in Makkah, and the more vulnerable he became. The only eminent non-Muslim supporter he could now rely on was Mut'im. Yet, those who remained in Makkah began to face even more bullying and persecution. Eventually, only the Prophet, Abu Bakr, and Ali remained in the city.

When Mut'im died in 622, the Prophet knew it was time to leave but awaited a sign from the Heavens before venturing to pack his bags. The news of his passing presented itself as an opportunity for the Quraysh. Finally, the day had come when Muhammad was now totally unprotected! Realizing this, the leaders of the Quraysh huddled together that night to hatch an evil plan.

"Decisive action needs to be taken to put a stop to Muhammad once and for all!" Utbah barked, pounding his fist on the wooden table.

"Exactly! His message is winning the foolish minds of far too many," Abu Jahl quickly added, trying to rouse up the men in the gathering.

A more relaxed and reasoning voice entered the conversation, though equally thrilled at the idea of harming the Prophet. "We must think about our children and *their* future." This was the voice of Qusay, the man hosting this meeting in his house. "If Muhammad were to join forces with the people of Yathrib, they could all end up attacking us, and we all know how skilled in warfare they are," he said as he played with his long moustache. He then stepped back into the shadows of the dimly lit room, only the menace flashing in his eyes now visible.

A man jolted out of his seat. "I propose we build a prison out of solid iron for him, lock him up in there, and throw away the key!" he proclaimed before sitting down, looking rather pleased with his idea and fully expecting to hear a round of applause.

He was instead met with criticism.

"What a ridiculous idea," drawled a low voice, commanding everyone's attention. "If you imprison him, his message will continue to spread beyond the cell walls. In fact, his followers will likely grow in number and will one day all return to rescue their so-called prophet, trampling over us in the process." The chilling words came from the devil disguised as a man standing near the shadowed walls. His sole intention was to steer the conversation to its most evil conclusion, and so he said suggestively, "We need something else—something better."

That night, Abu Jahl was not the most wicked person in the room. Too immersed in their scheming, no one bothered to question the identity of the mysterious yet compelling speaker as they murmured their agreement.

Abu Jahl decided to reveal his long-desired plan. "He's right. If we, the noble Quraysh, do not act fast, very soon our traders could be blocked from traveling to Syria for business as all routes pass through Yathrib. This would be a disaster beyond imagination. We must eliminate Muhammad!"

There was a moment's pause as a flicker of interest rippled across the room. Some men widened their eyes, nodding earnestly until a frowning Utbah spoke up.

"Assassination? There is a reason we have not gone that route in the first place."

At this, the assembly sobered, for although they supported the idea of doing away with Muhammad—his teachings contradicting their worldly lifestyle and tribal whims—something held them back. A major obstacle that was enough to make them resent their very own culture.

For many years it was impossible to simply kill Muhammad because he was protected by his uncle Abu Talib, and whoever killed him would face revenge from the powerful Hashim Tribe. Though not all of the tribespeople were Muslim or even supporters of Muhammad, the fact remained that Muhammad was still a tribe member and they would certainly avenge his death to protect the tribe's honour. Even though Muhammad's biggest supporter, Abu Talib, was now dead, the code of honour still existed. How could they get around this obstacle that protected him?

After debating several options, Abu Jahl proposed a plan that grabbed everyone's attention and alleviated their growing headache. "We shall all take part in this solution," he began, referring to murder as casually as if they were discussing what to eat. The men listened closely as he continued, "We will send a group of men to assassinate Muhammad in the night. A man from each tribe. With the crime shared between all tribes, no single person or tribe can be blamed."

This cunning plan would make a revenge attack extremely unlikely. They agreed on it straight away and raised their glasses of wine, invoking the names of Laat, Manaat, and Uzza—their three most revered gods. The scheming leaders of the Quraysh sank back in their seats, shoulders relaxing as they exchanged optimistic grins. Little did they know—they plan and Allah plans, and Allah is the best of all planners!

The Prophet was immediately alerted of their scheme by the angel Jibril. The Archangel then informed him that Allah had permitted him to leave for Yathrib.[39] The next day, the Prophet went to the house of Abu Bakr. His visit, at an unusual time, indicated the urgency of the news he had to share. He told Abu Bakr that the moment to leave Makkah had finally arrived. As the Prophet shared details of how they would escape that night, both excitement and worry began to run all over Abu Bakr's body in equal measure. This was not going to be easy.

That evening, while everyone in Makkah was asleep, assassins gathered with daggers and spears. Their goal was to ambush the Prophet on his way out for the dawn prayer or to answer the call of nature at any point in the night. Veiled by darkness, they surrounded the Prophet's house, each man poised at the ready, hoping to be the first to plunge their weapon into Muhammad when he would next leave, unaware that Allah had already revealed to him their plan.

Sensing their presence, the Prophet put his own plan into action. He gestured to Ali to come over and then whispered in his ear. "Sleep in my bed tonight and use my green robe as your blanket," he said. "Do not worry, they will not be able to harm you."

Ali, still a teenager, accepted this without protest. He loved the Prophet more than anything and knew that the promise of the Prophet would never be broken. Nevertheless, that night was not an easy one for young Ali. He lay awake under the covers, acutely aware that at any moment the door could be smashed in by the assassins should they tire of waiting. Indeed, the assassins were watching and had peered through the window to check if the Prophet had woken up. It appeared to them as though he was fast asleep. They had no idea that he was, in fact, just about to leave right under their noses.

The enemies had surrounded the entire house, covering every exit, window and door. How then would the Prophet get past them unnoticed? Without a shred of panic, Prophet Muhammad approached the door with full certainty that his greatest ally, Allah, would take care of him. As he stepped outside, he swiftly scooped up a handful of sand which he blew in the direction of the assassins while quietly reciting verses from the Qur'an. Though they had heard the unmistakable creak of the door, the assassins saw nothing out of the ordinary. Their eyes wildly scanned the rustling bushes in the front garden, seeing nothing—yet they were looking straight through him!

Allah had made the Prophet invisible to them so he was able to slip past completely undetected.

The Prophet headed straight to Abu Bakr's house, where his closest friend was waiting with two horses and supplies. The time to say goodbye to Makkah had finally come, just as Waraqa had predicted thirteen years ago. A gentle breeze blew across the sleeping city, the streets barely illuminated by the faint starlight. As the two of them crept out of the city, the Prophet turned to look at Makkah, his birthplace, for what seemed like the last time.

His voice held great pain as he said, "I swear that in the eyes of Allah, you are the best and most beloved place in the whole world. Had it not been for the fact that I am being forced to leave you, I would never have left."

He gazed upon the shadowed landscape of the home he loved, and then gently nudging his horse to take the lead, the two men set out on their journey. The momentous occasion of the Prophet's migration to Yathrib, soon to be named Madinah, had begun.

Just before the break of dawn, the assassins heard noises coming from inside the Prophet's house. Finally, the time had come to launch their attack. They readied themselves, positioning their weapons to strike fast and strike hard. The earliest rays of the slowly rising sun seeped into the window, casting a soft light into the room where their target stirred. The assassins froze. Their eyes widened, astonishment seizing their faces when they saw Ali rise from the Prophet's bed, the green robe slipping off to reveal his youthful face. Frustrated and annoyed, they realized they had been outsmarted. The assassins rushed off to inform the leaders, but by then, Prophet Muhammad and Abu Bakr had long since escaped Makkah.

To throw the enemies off their tracks, the two decided to head out south towards Yemen, even though Yathrib was in the opposite direction. Although the whole journey would now take twice as long, they felt that this would be a clever move. However, the Quraysh, fuelled by their convictions, were not going to give up that easily. That same morning, they made a public service announcement: Whoever could find Muhammad— dead or alive—would receive a reward of one hundred camels, equivalent to the wealth of a millionaire today! The huge bounty created a lot of commotion. As soon as the people heard, everybody wanted to get their hands on the reward.

The situation became increasingly dangerous as now the most well-trained hunters and warriors set off in hot pursuit of the two. Aware that the Quraysh could still track their footsteps, the Prophet and Abu Bakr went into hiding for a few days inside a cave in Mount Thawr, five miles south of Makkah. Abu Bakr's son, Abdullah, who was just a young boy at the time, had already been instructed to gather intelligence about the Quraysh's intentions by day and to bring it to them by night. Abu Bakr's daughters, Asma and Aisha, would prepare food and secretly carry it to the cave at night. When any of them would sneak out of Makkah, they took a small herd of sheep to cover their tracks. This is how the family of Abu Bakr supported the Prophet in his migration to Yathrib.

Despite all these precautions, a group of men from the Quraysh suspected that the two had taken a different route, and so they headed south to look for the Prophet. In no time at all, they approached Mount Thawr, soon noticing a cave big enough for one or possibly two people to hide inside. The men jumped off their horses and made their way up the mountain to the mouth of the cave. Before long, their approaching footsteps could be heard. The men, talking in hushed tones, were preparing to enter the cave.

Abu Bakr watched anxiously as their shadows began to creep in through the opening, casting elongated shapes across the dusty floor. A shudder ran down his spine, though he was not scared for his own life. What mattered most to him was that the Prophet was not harmed. The sound of unsheathing swords echoed into the cave. At that moment, Abu Bakr peered over and whispered to the Prophet, "O Messenger of Allah, if they were to just look down at their feet, they would spot us!"

To his surprise, the Prophet appeared as composed as ever, as though the enemy was not on the verge of discovering them. "Have no fear, for Allah is with us," the Prophet assured his Companion, before adding, "O Abu Bakr! Have you considered the fate of the two when the third with them is none other than Allah?"

At this, Abu Bakr understood. Allah was with them. A sense of peace and calmness washed over his heart. What happened next was nothing short of a miracle. The men who were about to raid the cave suddenly stopped in their tracks, seemingly preoccupied with something else. Abu Bakr watched as their shadows froze, their feet hesitating to take another step.

"If Muhammad were hiding in there, then this spiderweb, which must have taken days to spin, would surely have been disturbed," one of them mused aloud.

Elaborate silken threads covered the entrance of the cave, a solitary spider resting in the centre of the web, clearly undisturbed. The assassins deliberated this. After a brief back-and-forth, they then returned to their horses to continue the search elsewhere.

The two men hiding in the cave had escaped the clutches of their enemies by the narrowest of margins, all thanks to Allah. Their lives had been saved by nothing but a fragile spiderweb. This was the power of trusting in Allah that the Prophet had reminded Abu Bakr of. However, such lessons were not easy to master, as Abu Bakr would soon discover. The road to Yathrib was still a long way ahead.

Back in Makkah, a man named Suraaqa was sitting with his fellow tribesmen in the protective shade of the palm trees when a man came rushing over with urgent news. He skidded to a halt before the group of men, nearly knocking over the few clay pots that held their dates and water.

"Chief Suraaqa! I have seen two figures in a nearby valley and believe it to be Muhammad and his Companion!" he announced enthusiastically, grinning widely.

Before anyone could react, Suraaqa replied in a calm and casual tone, "You're mistaken. Rather you saw such-and-such people looking for their lost camel." He rattled off two random names without batting an eyelid, but despite his words, in his heart Suraaqa knew it was indeed them.

The man appeared somewhat deflated. "Well, perhaps you're right..." he said, his voice falling silent out of respect for the chief of the tribe. Discouraged, he realized he had been wrong for addressing Suraaqa so loudly in the first place. Suraaqa was twice as tall as most people and so huge that he easily parted crowds when he walked; he was not the kind of person one could approach so boldly.

Averting their attention from the sulking announcer, the group continued their conversations as though nothing had happened, unaware of Suraaqa's true intentions.

Now that he could pursue the two men without having to share the bounty, Suraaqa waited a few more moments before slipping away. Taking his fastest horse and sharpest spear, he made a beeline in the direction of his target. Suraaqa's horse galloped with determination that mirrored his own as it raced between dunes, lurching over the rocky outcrops that adorned the terrain. When he saw two figures in the distance, the excitement made him want to ride faster. He urged his horse to speed up, kicking his heels against its muscular body. Instead of catching up with them, he felt the front two legs of his horse begin to sink into the sand. The majestic creature then buckled, sending Suraaqa tumbling headlong onto the ground.

The bounty hunter narrowed his eyes as he lifted himself off the sand, using his spear for balance. This was certainly odd. None of his horses had ever done this before. Sensing that something mysterious was happening, he decided to turn to his pagan gods for guidance. The Arabs had a practice of using the tips of arrows marked with peculiar symbols to see into the future, much like the tarot cards of fortune-tellers today. If the arrow tips landed in a certain way, it would be a good sign, unless of course, it landed in another way, which would mean STOP RIGHT NOW.

The sign Suraaqa got was clear as daylight,[40] but the bounty of one hundred camels was too great for him to resist. He simply could not turn back. Driven by greed, Suraaqa stubbornly jumped back on his horse. Again he gave the two men chase. Abu Bakr, noticing the pursuing horseman drawing closer, kept looking over his shoulder. Grave concern was etched on his face. The distance between their horses and their pursuer was narrowing by the second. The Prophet remained calm, melodiously reciting verses from the Qur'an as though the bounty hunter was powerless to do anything.

When Suraaqa was close enough to hear the Prophet's recitation, his horse buckled again, sending him crashing to the ground. Disgruntled, he raised his head to see how far the two had gotten, but a mysterious curtain of dust appeared, preventing him from seeing their movement. Not willing to give up after so much effort, he mounted his horse for a second time, whipping it into an unrelenting gallop. Hearing the neighing of their enemy's horse, Abu Bakr found himself looking over his shoulder once more. When he realized the persistence of their pursuer, his eyebrows scrunched together in worry.

"O Messenger of Allah!" he shouted over the sound of hooves thumping the ground. "This man will surely catch us."

The reply from the Prophet was just like that in the cave. Composed. Unafraid. "Have no fear, Allah is with us." Once again, his words carried the weight of certainty.

Their horses continued ahead, manes whipping in the wind. When Suraaqa was just a few meters behind them, Abu Bakr became overwhelmed with emotion.

"Why do you cry?" the Prophet asked him, concerned.

Abu Bakr shook his head, using the tail-end of his turban to dry his tears. "I swear by God, I don't cry over me *but over you*."[41]

The Prophet's eyes glimmered with empathy as he looked at his friend, understanding the selflessness of his anxiety. At that moment, the Prophet raised his voice in a prayer that made Suraaqa drop the reigns of his horse.

"O Allah! Protect us from him in whichever manner you wish."

At this, Suraaqa felt his entire body become limp. All the signs he had seen up until now finally made sense. In a moment of clarity, he realized that these were no two ordinary men. It was clear that they were being protected by Allah, and that one day they would have great power and influence. Of this, Suraaqa was certain, this intuition taking root firmly in his heart.

"Please, offer me the promise of protection!" he called out to them at the top of his lungs, his voice carried by the wind.

The Prophet instructed Abu Bakr to allow their pursuer to catch up. When Suraaqa laid eyes on the Prophet it only confirmed his thoughts and he felt even more afraid for trying to kill such a noble man. Suraaqa was treated with such respect it caught him off guard. The Prophet sensed his change of heart, and much to Suraaqa's delight, his request was honoured. An official letter of protection was handed over to him.

Suraaqa stood with the letter clutched to his chest as he bid the two farewell, unaware that in the years to come, the significance of that letter would come to the fore in a very critical moment. How Allah had shaped the course of his fate was something to marvel over—Suraaqa had left his home bent on committing murderer, only later to seek protection from his would-be victims, before arriving home with a piece of paper that would one day save his own life. It was as though whoever crossed paths with the Prophet could expect to see a bright and unbelievable future beyond what they could even begin to predict.

A wild hawk flew overhead, its shadow sliding across the sun-soaked sand, overtaking the two men who slowed their horses to a steady trot. At last, the Prophet was out of the threatening reach of the Quraysh, and Abu Bakr had learned an invaluable lesson in the concept of *tawakkul* (trusting in Allah). The two made their way across the sweltering deserts of Arabia, knowing full well that though no soul was in sight, they were not alone.

> *We may never be forced to migrate from our homes to another foreign place for the sake of Allah, but there is another form of migration that we can do every day! When someone abstains from doing a sin or act of disobedience, they engage in a spiritual form of migration: migrating away from the displeasure of Allah to His pleasure.*

Bibliography

1. Ibn Ishaq- The Wüstenfeld's edition of *Sirat Rasul Allah*, a life of the Prophet by Muhammad ibn Ishaq in the annotated recension of 'Abd al-Malik ibn Hisham.

2. Ibn Sa'd- The Leyden edition of *Kitab at-Tabaqat al-Kabir* by Muhammad ibn Sa'd.

3. al-Tabari- *Tarikh al-Tabari* edited by Muhammad Abul Fadl Ibrahim, 2nd Edition, Printed by Daar al-Ma'arif.

4. Ibn Kathir- The Center for Muslim Contribution to Civilization edition of *As-Sīrah an-Nabawiyya*, The Life of Prophet Muhammad by Ibn Kathir.

Endnotes

1   Ibn Sa'd p. 28
2   As-Sīrah an-Nabawiyya by Ibn Kathir p. 26
3   Ibn Ishaq 102
4   Sahih Muslim, Hadith no. 162
5   As-Sīrah an-Nabawiyya by Ibn Kathir vol 1 p.169
6   Sahih Muslim, Hadith no. 976
7   Ibn Ishaq, p. 119
8   As-Sīrah an-Nabawiyya by Ibn Kathir vol 1 p. 175
9   As-Sīrah an-Nabawiyya by Ibn Kathir vol 1 p. 189
10   Ibn Ishaq, p. 120
11   Sahih al-Bukhari, Hadith no. 3
12   Ibn Ishaq, p. 153
13   Tarikh al-Tabari, vol 1 p. 533
14   Tarikh al-Tabari, vol 2 p. 298
15   Sahih al-Bukhari, Hadith no. 3
16   Sahih al-Bukhari, Hadith no. 3
17   Musad Imam Ahmad, Hadith no. 15033
18   Musnad Imam Ahmad, Hadith no. 3748
19   Sahih al-Bukhari, Hadith no. 3610
20   Sahih Muslim, Hadith no. 832
21   Tafsir Ibn Kathir. See verse 93 of Surah al-Hijr
22   As-Sīrah an-Nabawiyya by Ibn Kathir vol 1 p. 458
23   Ibn Ishaq p. 168
24   Ibn Sa'd, vol 4 p. 164
25   As-Sīrah an-Nabawiyya by Ibn Kathir vol 1 p. 326
26   As-Sīrah an-Nabawiyya by Ibn Kathir vol 1 p. 324
27   Ibn Ishaq p. 227
28   Ibn Ishaq p. 230
29   Sahih al-Bukhari, Hadith no. 7498
30   As-Sīrah an-Nabawiyya by Ibn Kathir vol 2 p. 84
31   As-Sīrah an-Nabawiyya by Ibn Kathir vol 1 p. 340
32   Ibn Ishaq p. 280
33   Ibn Ishaq p. 264
34   As-Sīrah an-Nabawiyya by Ibn Kathir vol 2 p. 65
35   Bukhari, Hadith no. 3430
36   Tirmidhi, Hadith no. 213
37   Ibn Ishaq p. 287
38   As-Sīrah an-Nabawiyya by Ibn Kathir vol 2 p. 133
39   Ibn Hisham vol 1 p. 482
40   As-Sīrah an-Nabawiyya by Ibn Kathir vol 2 p. 163
41   al-Bukhari, Hadith no. 3615